Bearing Witness

Bearing Witness

A Photographic Chronicle
of American Life,
1860-1945

Michael Lesy

With a preface by Warren I. Susman

Pantheon Books, New York

To André

———

Lesy, Michael, 1945-   Bearing witness.

Library of Congress Cataloging in Publication Data

1. United States–History–1865–1921–Pictorial works.

2. United States–History–Civil War, 1861–1865–Pictorial works.

3. United States–History–1919–1933–Pictorial works.

4. United States–History–1933–1945–Pictorial works.

5. United States–Description and travel–Views.

I. Title.

E661.L66   973   82-2297

ISBN 0-394-50967-6   AACR2

ISBN 0-394-74942-1 (pbk.)

Manufactured in the United States of America

First Edition

Grateful acknowledgment is made to the following for permission to reprint previously published material: (1) Harry N. Abrams, Inc.: Quotation as epigraph from *Treasures of the Library of Congress*, Charles A. Goodrum. Copyright © 1980 by Harry N. Abrams, Inc. Reprinted by permission of Harry N. Abrams, Inc. (2) Farrar, Straus & Giroux, Inc., and Jonathan Cape Ltd.: Quotation as epigraph from *Camera Lucida: Reflections on Photography* by Roland Barthes, trans. Richard Howard. Translation copyright © 1981 by Farrar, Straus & Giroux, Inc. Reprinted by permission of Hill and Wang, a division of Farrar, Straus & Giroux, Inc., and Jonathan Cape Ltd. (3) Harcourt Brace Jovanovich, Inc., and Jonathan Cape Ltd.: Quotation from *Illuminations* by Walter Benjamin, ed. by Hannah Arendt, trans. by Harry Zohn, 1978. Reprinted by permission of Harcourt Brace Jovanovich, Inc., and Jonathan Cape Ltd. (4) Liveright Publishing Co.: Quotation as epigraph from *The Art of the Moving Picture* by Vachel Lindsay, 1922. Reprinted by permission of Liveright Publishing Co. (5) Macmillan Publishing Co., Inc.: Selections from "Poetry" are reprinted with permission of Macmillan Publishing Co., Inc., from *Collected Poems of Marianne Moore*. Copyright 1935 by Marianne Moore. Renewed 1963 by Marianne Moore and T.S. Eliot.

———

Acknowledgments

For their advice and comfort:

Joseph Duffy, William and Linda Greider, Nick Lemann, Pearl Cleage Lomax, Toby and John Quitsland, Peter Relic, Susan Rosenberg, Tinka Tingle, Bryan Wilkins.

For their skill and assistance:

At Nexus—

Cathy Egan, John Friedman, John Kafer, John McWilliams, Michael Reagen.

At the Library of Congress—

Leroy Bellamy, Elizabeth Betz, Alan Fern, George Hobart, Mary Isam, Jerry Kearns, Bob Lisbeth, Gerald Maddox, Annette Melville, Norman Shaffer, Marita Stamey, William Younger.

At the National Archives—

Barbara Burger, Carol Marsh, Hugh Tahman, Joe Thomas, James Trumble, Bobbye West, Paul White, Dick Yuso.

Contents

Preface

It is the advent of the Photograph . . . which divides the history of the world.

Roland Barthes, 1981

In no other form of society in history have there been such a concentration of images, such a density of visual messages.

John Berger, 1972

There seems little doubt that our mental images of the past came from written descriptions for the first hundred years but from frozen pictorial descriptions for the second.

Charles A. Goodrum, 1974

American civilization grows more hieroglyphic every day. The cartoons of Darling, the advertisements in the back of magazines and on the billboards in streetcars, the acres of photographs in the Sunday papers, make us into a hieroglyphic civilization far nearer to Egypt than to England.

Vachel Lindsay, 1922

Historians have yet to confront fully the implications of America's becoming a "hieroglyphic" civilization. We have been living in a new world of visual images since the nineteenth century, with a range of consequences at least analogous to what occurred when civilization based on oral communication was transformed by the introduction of writing and, ultimately, printing. What is clear is the fundamental role of photography in our new world. Surely William M. Ivins, Jr., [*Prints and Visual Communication* (Cambridge, MA: Harvard, 1953), p. 134] is correct when he proposes that photography provided a "means to ocular awareness of things that our eyes can never see directly." For him, photography was a "complete revolution in the way we use our eyes" and even more importantly "in the kind of things our minds permit our eyes to tell us." Such a revolution must certainly have had social and especially psychological consequences, but our cultural historians have scarcely begun to probe them.

This point is all the more significant because the advent of photog-raphy and the creation of this new world of images coincide with and are clearly related to other major cultural changes. The world of the photograph, for example, is also the world of everyday life—the quotidian the French sociologist Henri Lefebre analyzes with such brilliance in his *Everyday Life in the Modern World*. For not only is the concept of everyday life a product of the nineteenth century, but it is not unreasonable to suggest that the photograph, able to capture in exceptional detail the data of everyday life, made us aware of the role of the quotidian. The history of photography is the history of the revealing of the nature of everyday life; the history of the quotidian itself can exist only because the history of photography fundamentally documents it.

But the era of the photograph is also the era of our developing consumer culture. The consumption of images (as well as the more often-stressed images of consumption) is crucial to an understanding of that culture. For it is not hyperbole to suggest that photographs may very well be considered among the first items of "mass consumption." The astounding growth in the sheer number of professional photographers (less than 1,000 by 1850 and more than 20,000 by 1890) and the development of large commercial firms in the business of selling images suggest a special and important role photography played in the new consumer culture. While documentary photography functioned in the service of government agencies (like the Department of the Interior) or the new corporations (like the railroads), the overwhelming number of images taken were purchased by a hungry new middle-class consumers' market. By 1860 the "family album" had become a commonplace in middle-class homes. Photographers supplied the pictures and the albums grew over the years. There, alongside the family Bible (which often contained the family genealogy), the album became an extension of the Bible: a family history. Members of the family—perhaps, especially, the children—studied this important history *through* the photographs. The album provided another kind of history, another vision of development and change over time.

Family life often centered on other kinds of images as well. For photography provided for the first time a vast number of diverse views of the world outside the home. "I think there is no parlor in America where there is not a stereoscope," commented one mid-nineteenth-century German authority on photography visiting the United States. Certainly, by the time of the Civil War, photographic studios offered and consumers eagerly purchased all kinds of pictures documenting that war, for example. It is worth quoting at some length part of an advertisement Alex Gardner (whose work as a photographer you can see in this book) placed in a newspaper in 1863:

Photographic Incidents of the War

The largest and finest collection of War Views ever made. Apart from the great interest appertaining to them, they stand unequalled as works of art. Amongst the contributors will be found the names of some of the most distinguished Photographers in the country.

The collection consists chiefly of views and scenes on the battlefields of the first and second Bull Run, Yorktown, Fair Oaks, Savage Station, Cedar Mountain, Hilton Head, Fort Pulaski, South Mountain, Harper's Ferry, Antietam, and Fredericksburg. Views of Warrenton, Culpeper, Fairfax, Beaufort, Aquia Creek, Falmouth, Sharsburg, Berlin, Ruins of Hampton, and various interesting localities.

Groups of General Officers and Staffs. Groups illustrating Camp Life. Portraits of General Officers on Horseback. A large collection of distinguished personages, Military, Literary, and Scientific.

A corps of artists constantly in the field, who are adding to the collection daily.

Send for a catalog, corrected till 1st June 1863.

[Quoted in Robert Taft, *Photography and the American Scene* (New York: 1938), p. 231]

This is enough to suggest that the Civil War was the first great media event in American history. The vast photographic coverage of every aspect of the war was to fill, in 1911, ten volumes of *The Photographic History of the Civil War*. These images were purchased individually and in sets by thousands of American consumers during the war itself. Family life in the new consumer society therefore devolved around these images of the world as well as around private family images. The consequence of this fact has yet to be assessed.

Consumer culture finds its very base in the phenomenon of advertising. In the most literal sense, photographs—and many other of the new visuals—serve as advertisements. For the photographs do call attention to, give notice of, admonish and instruct, inform, give orders, or regulate, or even (in the most modern usage of the term) serve as paid announcements. This is no word game; rather, unless photographs are in fact examined as advertisements in the dictionary sense of the word, a major cultural function of these images will not be revealed.

Photographs are able to function as advertisements in our consumer culture because they also fulfill other needs so characteristic of American culture in the period since the middle of the nineteenth century. Emerson once suggested that Americans required both dreams and mathematics. Certainly that rings true, most especially, for the United States by the turn of the century. There was always the demand for the real, for Mr. Gradgrind's hard facts. Social survey, empirical data, statistics, fictional realism, science, solid flesh, a material universe, on the one hand; fairies and fairy tales, folklore, flights of fancy, extravaganzas, magic transformations, dreams and nightmares, spiritualism, and idealism, on the other. The complication culturally was not in the conflict between two orders but the insistence on both at the same time: dreams *and* mathematics, as Emerson suggested. So L. Frank Baum, the great inventor of the Land of Oz, argued for realistic fairy stories. This, in effect, symbolizes the consumer culture in its ideal form. And the photograph—the agency of science that recorded hard fact—was also the vehicle of magic transformations and the unseen world. Marianne Moore once defined a poem as an "imaginary garden with real toads in it." But that is precisely what a photograph is: Cut off in space from whatever unknown world surrounds it, frozen forever in time, the photograph is set in a never-never land, isolated and floating like any fairy tale, any dream; yet within that frame, arbitrary or fancy-free as it may be, there are those "real toads," the fundamental data, the hard facts. Thus, the photograph itself is defined by those very tensions that in most significant ways are the tensions of the culture itself. "The age demanded an image," the poet announced [in Ezra Pound's *Hugh Selwyn Mauberley*]. And the images that the various ages of the era of consumer culture demanded were often most significantly to be found in photographs. In the very last paragraphs of his monumental study of some of man's fundamental myths in *The Golden Bough* (1890), Sir George Frazer offered the hope that "the dreams of magic may one day be the waking reality of science." That may be a key idea of the consumer culture and an important view of what many in that culture saw photography as achieving.

The coming of photography was thus a major event in history; perhaps an event of special import because it forced a change in our thinking about history itself. Early authorities on photography were certain this was the case: "Posterity, by the agency of photography, will view the faithful image of our times; the future students, in turning the pages of history, may at the same time look on the very skin, into the very eyes, of those long since mouldered to dust, whose lives and deeds he traces in the text." [Lake Price (1858) quoted in Taft, *Photography and the American Scene*, p. 137.] But a more recent student raises the issue of history and the photograph in a different and more sophisticated context. Granted, the photograph overcomes the resistance to believing in the past (with the photograph "the past is as certain as the present"). But this is not because the photograph succeeds simply as a representation of a previous reality. "The important thing is that the photograph possesses an evidential force, and that its testimony bears not on the object but on time. . . . The power of authentication exceeds the power of representation." [Roland Barthes, *Camera Lucida* (New York: Hill and Wang, 1981), pp. 88-89.]

Bearing Witness probes that special relationship between the past and photography, or, perhaps more significantly, between history and the photograph. Early in our own century scholars and critics began to examine these relationships, to analyze our culture in terms of its more popular cultural artifacts, to take seriously our photographic heritage. Notice has already been taken of the ten-volume *Photographic History of the Civil War* published in 1911. It was also in this period that the Library of Congress itself began to develop seriously and systematically its great collections of photographs. And it was in these early decades of the century as well that more and more serious effort turned to the analysis of images and their significance. For example, a new poetics announced the centrality of "the image": ". . . that which presents an intellectual and emotional complex in an instant of time." In the same essay ("A Few Don'ts by an *Imagiste*," *Poetry*, March 1913), Ezra Pound insisted on "direct treatment of

the 'thing,' whether subjective or objective," and warned against "abstractions." Although Pound claimed music as his guide, much of this sounds as if it were derived from the new world of visual images and especially the photograph. But as late as 1940 students of documentary photography were still trying to find the way toward full historical use of these "documents" and still seeking the subtler relationships between photography and history. In their article in the American Historical Association volume *The Cultural Approach to History*, Roy Stryker and Paul H. Johnstone reviewed the major photographic sources and urged historians to participate in their use. But what they largely found in the photographs were "physical details of material culture," "clues to social organization and institutional relationships," and, finally, a rather vague suggestion that such photographs "can interpret the human and particularly the inarticulate elements."

The serious work of the last quarter century in photography and cultural history has brought us to a point where we can really begin to understand the relationship between photography and history. Arranging photographs carefully as products of a culture and therefore related to one another, the analyst can explore more firmly the psychological underpinnings and the social and cultural relationships now revealed. The very form (the photograph) helps not only as a representation of simple material facts and documented events but also as a reflection of the culture from which it comes, an authentication of its tensions, its confusions, its paradoxes, its psychological as well as social victories and defeats, its vision of itself, its self-consciousness. History has always been the story of the development of self-awareness over time; in our era the photograph has become, for all the reasons suggested above, a major instrument for recording that growing self-consciousness.

A few examples of a reading of this vision in Michael Lesy's collection are in order. Note that Lesy allows no traditional heroism in any of his Civil War photographs. There is a special haunted sense in almost every frame. This is a war of profound moral difficulties; the victors fail to look victorious. Alex Gardner's "General Caldwell and staff on the battlefield of Antietam," (1-11) can speak for others in the group. Here the traditional staff grouping does not result in a traditional view. Virtually every face appears mad, driven insane, haunted by horror. The flag is most casually draped; there is little that speaks of God or country. The Black in the background appears almost as an accusing ghost. But the extraordinary nature of this image—an image that is virtually a self-conscious condemnation of the very war it seems to celebrate—is even more apparent when compared to a contemporary parallel photograph such as one of Roger Fenton's Crimean War photographs (the Library of Congress also has a major collection of these photographs). Fenton's officers and staff pose romantically and heroically. They gesture with dramatic effect. The uniforms, the flags, the tents are neat and orderly; the backgrounds free of any disorder or any threatening ghosts. It is too simple to argue that Fenton is an "unrealistic" photographer. Is he not in fact creating the image they want at home in England? But what of Gardner, that seller of images? Who would want his mad vision and why? Does that not tell us something profoundly true about the moral and psychological ambivalence of Americans about their Civil War?

Or the images in Black Life: How can "Romeo and Juliet" (p. 23) and Frances Benjamin Johnston's seated woman (p. 24) both be said to be "representative" of Black life? Of course, they represent, rather, two vastly different perceptions, perceptions that can and do dwell side by side in the same American universe. History informs us that Alfred Campbell's image ("Romeo and Juliet") is the more typical as well as stereotypical, the image perhaps most Americans wished to believe. But at the same time Johnston's images not only inform us of history's too often forgotten alternative visions but alert us in the present to the possibilities of our own options.

And Lewis Hine's incredible children? Each precious and sentimental child reveals both the "real" (that is, surface image) and the "ideal" (the angel hidden inside). Hine sees no evil in his "sitters." The photographs actually show us perhaps not what *was* but always exactly what Hine *sees*. His remains a vision of pre-Freudian innocence, no matter how the dirt and toil discolored skin and bone. The question is not whether or not these images represent what is real but rather what in fact the basic reality is. For Hine and many "progressives" as well, remove the dirt and toil and the basic and real goodness does shine through.

And what of the strange intruder who interrupts the carefully posed and rather pompous Signal Corps group (p. 67)? What reason or right permits the native Filipino to pop his head in the window and spoil the shot? Or does that incredible juxtaposition somehow reveal the reality of the imperial situation? And what of Frances Benjamin Johnston's Marine officer (p. 71)? Does it really give you historical information? What data does it offer? What facts about America? There, with all the neat and patient composition, the beauty of the flowers in the foreground; the elegance of the perfectly draped flag; the precision of the tent; the care of the framing; the tall, immaculately dressed and handsome officer—and yet somehow deep within the picture itself some awful mystery, some hidden horror? There is a seemingly enormous black spot, a hole of darkness without end at the very center of the picture. How many dark spots are there at the very heart of these American pictures Lesy presents? What does that tell us about America as the century turned? This seems especially the case when this picture is placed beside the several sentimental stereos or any of the other "soft-porn" stereos on pp. 72 and 73. The arrangement of images, the forced comparison that photographs not only make possible, because of the overwhelming abundance of images (a charac-

teristic of an age of abundance, a consumer culture), but insist upon. Images tumble one upon the other; a kind of montage occurs in which the conflict among images suddenly reveals a cultural conflict behind all the images and more serious than any single image can portray.

Or the "Farm woman feeding her pullets" (p. 99) who wears one of her Sunday dresses to undertake a chore she would probably never do in that particular dress. Undoubtedly, she does it because she was being photographed and was clearly delighted with that fact. So we immediately are reminded that the fact of photographing means not only a conscious perspective on the part of the photographer but also one on the part of his subject—a kind of double Heisenberg effect. Yet, while that fact casts doubt on some historical accuracy (that dress for feeding pullets), it tells us at the same time another important fact: A farm woman in 1927 has a special sense of pride and wants to be seen in her best dress—a psychological and sociological truth of some importance. And how much we learn from a comparison of dress between family members. "Farmer and his family" (p. 104) appears a simple enough family group, but a careful examination of differences in clothing styles (especially in the generations of women) appears to reveal other significant differences as well, both psychological and moral.

Many of the photographs illustrating the Depression end up even more impressively demonstrating ideological difficulties in coping with the victims of the Depression. For years, I have experimented with Farm Security Administration photographs in classes. If the class knows nothing about the New Deal and the aims and purposes of the FSA, and if the photographs are presented without their captions, I can usually anticipate one response; when the captions are revealed, the response almost always changes. For many of these photographers found themselves both attracted to their subjects and yet anxious to dramatize their plight. They sought to make them victims and heroes at the same time. The captions often say what the photograph itself cannot reveal. Rothstein's Missouri "Evicted sharecropper and his child" (p. 113) certainly shows a concerned father and his child. But there is a strength, a beauty, a determination in the father's face, a sense of protectiveness toward the child that gives no clue to his troubles. He is heroic rather than beaten. Both of Dorothea Lange's pictures (pp. 108 and 109) are captioned "An aged cotton farmer who inherited his lands, which are heavily mortgaged now." This caption gives us information unavailable in the photographs themselves; yet, do the pictures in fact tell us the same thing? Once again, the point is not that the photographs do not give a true or a real picture. Rather, many of these pictures reveal other psychological "facts" or other "sociological" truths. Any study, for example, of the FSA photographs reveals a good deal about 1930s ideology and ideals, about 1930s visions and world view. Russell Lee shows us a "Migrant family saying grace before their noon-day meal by the side of the road" (p. 111). His caption tell us so. And every word of the caption is important. This is not simply a family picnic (although it certainly might have been). That very contrast is important: It tells us how the official New Deal wanted others to see and feel the world. These are significant advertisements as are all great pictures created for the consumption of Americans. Overall, the whole series of photographs suggests an astounding juxtaposition of images of abundance, achievement, and wealth, which one expects to discover in a consumer culture, with images of death, decay, disruption. Are these, too, characteristics of a consumer culture?

One last comment on these particular images Lesy has selected and arranged. His own vision of America's vision has led him to stress images of the wounded, the despairing, the damaged, and the confused. Many of these images are painful; some even horrible. Terror haunts this work as it haunted those Civil War participants, especially the terror of war and the organization of war. Often, Lesy appears a kind of Goya showing us ironically not his own visions of war but *our* own (those we consume regularly throughout our history). There is special warrant for these images in our tradition. As far back as 1756 Edmund Burke, staunch and conservative rationalist that he was, wrote *A Philosophical Inquiry into the Origins of Our Ideas of the Sublime and the Beautiful.* His vision of the sublime—a key idea in modern capitalist culture—is an important one to consider when viewing the images to which I have referred.

Whatever is fitted in any sort to excite the ideas of pain and danger, that is to say, whatever is in any sort terrible, or is conversant about terrible objects, or operates in a manner analogous to terror, is a source of the sublime; that is, it is productive of the strongest emotion which the mind is capable of feeling.

This is important to Burke because he wants all to seek their own self-preservation. He is convinced that the sublime, because of the strength of that emotion, will, through terror, produce that desired end. And so, too, Michael Lesy. He has given us a moral tale in his history. He has warned us against ourselves, using our own images, those images our age demanded, arranging them to form a new critical vision. From the images he has selected he has in fact constructed a History, always probing the relationship between our history and the images themselves. In the process, he has not only provided us with a vision of our past but forced us to clarify the issue of our own relationship to the images that have made our past. Thus, he has not only tried to illuminate the past that historians study but also tried to change our past that keeps unfolding through the present and into the future. Lesy is thus in a great tradition. He believes that a critical awareness of History can alter history itself. He has ordered our way through the new world of images, helping make sense of our "hieroglyphic" civilization in the hope that our new self-awareness can make us demand far different images and therefore live far different lives.

———

Warren I. Susman

Introduction

Theses on the Philosophy of History

I X

Mein Flügel ist zum Schwung bereit,
ich kehrte gern zurück,
denn blieb ich auch lebendige Zeit,
ich hatte wenig Glück.

Gerhard Scholem, *"Gruss vom Angelus"*

A Klee painting named "Angelus Novus" shows an angel looking as though he is about to move away from something he is fixedly contemplating. His eyes are staring, his mouth is open, his wings are spread. This is how one pictures the angel of history. His face is turned toward the past. Where we perceive a chain of events, he sees one single catastrophe which keeps piling wreckage upon wreckage and hurls it in front of his feet. The angel would like to stay, awaken the dead, and make whole what has been smashed. But a storm is blowing from Paradise; it has got caught in his wings with such violence that the angel can no longer close them. This storm irresistibly propels him into the future to which his back is turned, while the pile of debris before him grows skyward. This storm is what we call progress.

Walter Benjamin, *Illuminations*

There was once an old man who had the eyes and curiosity of a child. His name was Vanderbilt. His mother was a woman of considerable intelligence and beauty. His father was an artist who made a living, before the Great War, by traveling through Switzerland on behalf of the State Railways, making sketches of every charming station he encountered. His son, Paul, eventually became a librarian, but of a most peculiar sort, since he claimed to be as much interested in the analysis of images as in the cataloguing of ideas. Fifty years ago he began to investigate the problems of what is now called information storage, access, and retrieval—problems that had nothing in common except that, in each case, intelligent human activity had generated immense quantities of disparate, nonlinear data that somehow had to be organized so that in the future it could be used to decide questions of policy and taste. Thus, in 1938, Paul went to Holland, where he studied the information storage and retrieval methods developed by the Royal Dutch Shell Oil Company to assimilate the vast, heterogeneous, and ever-changing varieties of data generated by investment and exploration. From Holland, he went to Germany, where in Leipzig he nearly drowned in the *Deutsche Bucherei*, the central depository of everything, from matchbook covers to physics monographs, ever printed in Germany since the middle of the nineteenth century. Soon afterward, he was at work in Philadelphia, making a photographic inventory of every object in the Philadelphia Museum of Art and dreaming of something called "total access to total information."

By 1942, he had moved to Washington D.C., where his task was to organize the 250,000 photographs of American life made during the

Depression by photographers of the Farm Security Administration, under the direction of a former Columbia University economics instructor. Vanderbilt chose to divide the quarter million images into groups, first according to their geographic origin and then according to a set of activities believed to be common to all mankind. He derived this analytic strategy from that of the Yale Human Relations Area File, which was a comparative classification of the customs and beliefs of 150 human cultures, established in 1936 by Yale's department of anthropology.

When, during the Second War, the images of the Farm Security Administration were transferred to the Library of Congress, Vanderbilt went with them. Since there was no one else with either his training, experience, or omniverous curiosity, he became the first chief of the Library's photographic section, which was composed not only of Farm Security files but also of huge quantities of images of every conceivable description that had, until the early twentieth century, been deposited in the Library for copyright purposes by every American manufacturer of postcards, stereographs, advertisements, sentimental views, and *cartes de visite*.

In 1945, when Luther Evans, a Princeton political scientist, was the Librarian of Congress, Vanderbilt wrote an interoffice memo arguing that "if folklore is . . . in the broadest sense . . . the sum of man's irrational actions, all the charming products of imagination rather than science—language, symbols, games—then photography is one of the best tools for its examination" (from "A Program for the Care of Photographs in the Library of Congress," pp. 8–9, unpublished typescript, June 1945). For years, he sifted through warehouses full of prints, photographs, and posters confiscated by American forces in Nazi Germany and shipped to Washington as spoils of war. During the early fifties, at the request of the state department, he did nothing else for two years but research and organize a complete iconography of Iran. Again and again, over a period of eight years, he explored the Library's morass of American images, shaping the collection as if it were a work of art, a painting of paintings, a book of books, cross-indexed so as to allow researchers to pursue whatever free associations were inspired by the implicit content of a set of images. On Monday mornings, his colleagues often found him sleeping at his work table, collapsed over a pile of images he had been ordering and re-ordering all weekend.

In 1955, he completed a guide to the Library's photographic collections, and this remained the definitive work on the subject for twenty-five years. Sometime in the sixties, he moved to Wisconsin, where he went to work for the state historical society in Madison. He organized a department of iconography, where he proceeded to go on the same journeys and play the same games he had enjoyed in Washington. One hot, quiet afternoon, I met him by accident. He was

sitting all alone in his office, listening to a Janis Joplin record. We started talking and didn't stop for two years. He was the first one to tell me about the millions of photographs in the Library of Congress.

The archivists, librarians, and research assistants who presently compose the staff of what is now called the Prints and Photographs Division of the Library believe they have access, through their catalogue, to fifteen million images, or, as they say, "items." Like the gamekeepers of a preserve, they're quick to add that that's not how many items there actually are in the collection, that's just how many they've been able to tag and set loose again. There are herds of images without numbers, in hibernation on shelves in a sub-basement underneath an annex, and there are cold-storage sheds full of packing cases stuffed with them in the Maryland suburbs. Ten years ago, a recluse died and left the Library 60,000 images made during fifteen years of solitary wanderings through the streets of New York. Fourteen years ago, a whole newspaper went bankrupt and left the one and a quarter million images that comprised its picture morgue to the Library. Twelve years ago, a famous photographer of the rich, the well-born, and the able retired and placed 300,000 negatives and prints of her subjects in the Library's safekeeping. There's one collection alone—the remains of an extinct magazine—composed of five million images, but its reproduction rights have been in litigation so long that the curators simply acknowledge it and then warn the curious away, the same way that investigators at the Environmental Protection Agency might take note of a toxic-waste site as big as New Jersey. Every year, living people and organizations, or their survivors and executors, express their belief in the ultimate judgment of history by putting the pictures of their lives in cartons and sending them to the Library.

The archivists, research assistants, and clerks who preside over still pictures at the National Archives believe they have records of perhaps five million images. Every government agency ever created by executive or legislative fiat has spawned images during times of war and peace, and then, when they no longer believe them to be useful or incriminating, they cart them to the Archives. There they remain, with numbers on their backs, filed in "record groups" housed in stack levels called "decks," behind doors whose locks are frequently changed, while record officers nervously keep track of changing administrations and shifts in the Freedom of Information Act. On the outside, the Archives appears to be a shrine built of limestone, with fine words about the past and future cut into its cornices. On the inside, except for the space in which the Constitution and Declaration of Independence are displayed, it is more like an immense filing cabinet whose drawers are crammed with the remnants of meetings, strictures, inquiries, and directives. There are so many images in so many record groups whose content is either so banal or, occasionally, so horrific that they are often left undisturbed for years by anyone but the staff. The researcher who is allowed to walk through the stacks under supervision sometimes has the uneasy feeling that at night, when the images are left even more to themselves than during the day, they pass through a metamorphosis. Thus, just as nitrate negatives spontaneously combust under certain conditions of heat and humidity, so, in isolation, photographs of every post office in Maryland may slowly change into images of every land-reclamation project in Colorado, and these, in turn, may slowly transform themselves into pictures of every naval-supply depot in California.

Although there is a card catalogue that provides some insight into various photographic record groups, it is the archivists themselves who, for years, have kept track of the images that became, for the researcher, the equivalent of the renegades in Bradbury's *Fahrenheit 451.* But instead of this one's having committed *Anna Karenina* to memory, or that one's alone being able to recite the whole of *Don Quixote,* the research staff at the Archives have memorized such entities as the 250,000 images in the U.S. Navy collection or the 170,000 images in the U.S. Army Signal Corps, American Expeditionary Force collection.

Ten years ago, I walked through one of the Archive's decks for the first time. The air was cold, the ceilings low, the aisles narrow. The boxes of images were stacked five shelves high in cases that went on and on—as dense, endless, and dangerous to a vessel of ordinary memory as the Great Barrier Reef. During the tour, I had become as bored, restless, and uneasy as a five-year-old in a museum. Then my guide stopped, reached for a box from a shelf, and pulled a picture from it the way a dealer might cut a queen from a deck. He showed me the picture. Perhaps he had done this many times before. He said, "Do you know who this is?" He said "is," not "was." I said, "No." He said, "That's Halsey on Peleliu." It was a picture of a group of men in clean uniforms, climbing a sand dune pitted with shell holes. I looked at it. I was so numbed by the endless boxes, and the picture itself was so banal, that I nodded but said nothing. Then my guide said, "Look at his face." Halsey looked as if he were panting, out of breath. My guide said, "It was the bodies. That was a bad one. They were stinking and he caught a whiff." And that's when I thought, "Maybe there's a way to master this."

One way to master such data is to investigate its context; that is, in order to comprehend why a U.S. admiral was walking on the beach of a Pacific island breathing through his mouth, it may be necessary to understand that the battle for Peleliu, which began in the fall of 1944, resulted in an unprecedented number of casualties (10,000 Americans and 10,700 Japanese), and that these casualties were the result of a fatal three-part coincidence. The first was the erroneous American belief that Peleliu was lightly defended and that its relatively easy capture would be a strategic prelude to MacArthur's reconquest of the Philippines. The second was a fundamental change in Japanese tactics:

On Peleliu, for the first time during the war, Japanese officers were ordered by their superiors and instructed their men to die for the emperor, not in banzai charges but in counterattacking from deep dugouts and heavily armored, well-sited pillboxes. The third coincidence was the fatigue and inadequate prewar equipment of the attacking U.S. Marines, who had barely recovered from Guadalcanal and who were either blown out of the water or cut to pieces while trying to dig foxholes in solid limestone and coral.

But even a tactical and strategic understanding of the battle does not explain the expression on Halsey's face in the photograph my guide plucked from the box. The guide claimed that Halsey was breathing through his mouth to avoid the stink of corpses, while I, who knew little about the Pacific campaigns of World War II, and nothing about the battle of Peleliu, thought the middle-aged officer, whom I did not recognize, was panting from fatigue. Some insight is offered by kinesic psychology, a discipline that, in the past thirty years, has investigated human facial expression, posture, and gesture through the painstaking analysis of still photographs and freeze-frame motion pictures and video tape. Some of this discipline's most thorough research has occasionally been supported by such diverse patrons as the U.S. Department of State, the National Institute of Mental Health, and the Advanced Research Projects Agency of the defense department, perhaps because the ability to read the face as if it were a book is useful not only to gamblers but to diplomats, as well as to analysts evaluating data derived by covert surveillance. Whatever the sources of support for some of its more insightful research, the discipline's theoretical lineage can be traced from William Sheldon (who in 1942 claimed to have discovered a 60-to-80 percent correlation between body type and personality, and who proposed the provocative idea that the unconscious *is* the body), through Charles Darwin (his 1872 *Expression of Emotions in Man and Animals*), back to 1804 and the physiognomy of Levater, and beyond that to the art of Titian, Raphael, and Antonello de Messina, who believed that a painted portrait was a direct statement about the personality of the sitter. At present, kinesic psychologists and physiologists believe that the human face is capable of 20,000 different expressions, but that of those 20,000, expressions of happiness, sadness, anger, fear, disgust, and surprise are common to and are capable of being visually understood by all mankind, even though the occasions and situations for the display of such expressions vary from culture to culture.

Such insights, provided by a knowledge of historical context and psychology—especially if that knowledge is accompanied by a familiarity with other lateral disciplines that, if combined, can reveal the invisible lineaments of meaning in which a photograph is enmeshed—may provide researchers with some objective clarity during their investigations. But this still does not explain how researchers, when confronted not by one photograph but by tens or hundreds of thousands of them, can keep their objectivity; and it still does not explain how and why such objectivity is often lost or what replaces it once it is gone.

The best way to answer these questions is to begin with a *koan,* or riddle, told by a thirteenth-century Zen master called Ekai, who collected a number of them in an anthology entitled *No Gate Barrier* [*Zen Flesh, Zen Bones,* transcribed by Nyogen Senzaki and Paul Reps (Garden City, NY: Anchor Books, 1957), p. 114]. Here is the riddle, which is very brief: "Two monks were arguing about a flag. One said, 'The flag is moving.' The other said, 'The wind is moving.' The sixth patriarch happened to be passing by. He told them, 'Not the wind, not the flag; mind is moving.'"

The point is that the mind is moved by its own winds—winds of involuntary recollection, imagination, and unacknowledged desire. It is to still that movement, to quiet its restless pacings, to discover where one ends and the world *out there* begins that some people retreat behind the walls of monasteries and nunneries. To engage in historical research rather than contemplation, to investigate hundreds of thousands of items of visual data rather than to meditate in silence on a single transcendental moment . . . are these such antithetical activities? In fact, the investigation of vast quantities of sensory data is often as solitary an endeavor as the contemplation of a religious object or ideal. The enforced silence that surrounds a novice can be just as deafening as the howling, whistling chaos of information that surrounds a researcher. The sensory deprivation of contemplation and the sensory overload of photographic research can both result in the common mind taking leave of itself. Like Pip, the cabin boy in *Moby Dick,* who fell out of a whaleboat during a hunt, and who, while waiting to be rescued, went mad because he was left alone in the midst of the sea—so, at a certain point in either research or meditation, the novice and the historian risk their ordinary sanity, surrounded by an infinity of silence or an infinity of information. At that moment, what the novice involuntarily "sees" is his own mortal self—that hungry little creature that seeks the light and fears the cold—and, at a parallel moment, what the visual historian involuntarily understands is his own fearful prejudices and hopes, which, until then, had clouded his sight.

Every month, for eighteen months, I traveled between my home in Atlanta and the photographic collections in Washington. Each month, for five days, eight hours a day, I looked at photographs. At the end of one week, I counted the number of images I had looked at. I discovered I'd examined 70,000 of them. I'm sure there are those who, reading this, are skeptical of my arithmetic. But the review and evaluation of a great number of images is no more or less difficult than the running of a long-distance race. Beyond a preparatory knowledge of history and psychology, there are three things required of anyone engaged in the investigation of large quantities of sensory data: The first is the ability to pass through a kind of boredom, caused by fatigue, into a state of wakeful dreaming during which one is both alert and passive, as during actual sleep; the second is the ability to remember the images that pass before one's eyes—images that are the actual pictures being scanned very rapidly, and images that are briefly provoked in one's imagination by the photographs themselves and that are composed of the same stuff as dreams; the third is the ability to tolerate and consciously assimilate the irrational hopes and fears elicited by the sensory stimuli of the photographs and that emerge as spontaneously as laughter from a child who is ticklish. This entire effort is a balancing act between a state of critically disinterested *intellectual* understanding and a state of open, spontaneous *sensory* and *emotional* engagement. Such a balance is difficult to achieve but even more difficult to maintain, since the representational nature of the data causes one's own irrationality to emerge like a sudden gust of wind that can threaten the safety of a high-wire act.

For example, toward the end of my research, I examined several thousand images, made by U.S. Army and civilian photographers, of German concentration camps liberated by U.S. troops in 1945. My first intellectual encounter with these camps and their liberation occurred when I was fourteen years old. That year, I had traveled to Israel, and one night I met people who my parents told me were my cousins. There were twenty of them, eating cake and drinking wine at a long table in a bare room, in a wretched house on an unpaved road of dust outside of Tel Aviv. My cousins were short, dark, and middle-aged. They laughed and shouted in Russian and Yiddish, which I could not understand. The man who sat next to me showed me a photograph. He held it in front of me and explained it to my father, who told me what he said. It was a picture of eight or nine men and women, standing in the snow in a clearing. They were all armed. Their weapons were pointed at the camera. My father told me that, during the war, my cousins had survived as partisans between the Russian and German lines. I asked who took the picture. My cousin said, "A German. We captured him, he took the picture, and then we shot him." Between the time I was fourteen and the time I was thirty-five, I had seen other pictures of the war in Europe and the Holocaust, and had read many accounts, both literary and scholarly, of those events. But, until the morning I walked into the still pictures branch of the National Archives and asked one of the staff to bring me images from the camps, the closest I had ever come to that catastrophe was the picture my cousin in Tel Aviv had held in his hands.

That morning in the Archives, I believed myself to be intellectually and emotionally prepared to examine whatever images I might encounter. During the course of my research, I had seen images of death made during the Civil War, the First War, the island battles of World War II. I had seen pictures of men, animals, buildings, and land twisted and cratered in ways I had never imagined. When the research assistant rolled out a metal cart stacked with boxes, I believed I could bear the sight of another human disaster. The first box I opened was the largest. It contained 16″ × 20″ prints—images so large that they filled my field of vision. As soon as I opened the box, everything changed. One minute, the air was calm and the room was quiet. The next, it was as if I had walked in front of the open mouth of a furnace called a glory hole, where glass is kept in a molten state. On either side of such a furnace, the air is neither visible nor tangible. But in front of it, the air roars, twists, and tears as if it were water shooting from a flame.

For the next five days, I returned, first to the Archives, then to the Pentagon, to examine the images. I began to think that, just as there were divine miracles during which, Hume said, the laws of nature were temporarily suspended, so there were satanic ones. I began to think that I was witnessing such a miracle, and that this knowledge was something I could not bear. I began to read the Prophets, all of whom had seen what they had seen not because they'd wanted to, and all of whom had said what they'd said not because they had had any choice. During the early twentieth century, scholars had wondered if these prophets were lunatics feeding on their own hallucinations, or poets caught up in the sound of their own voices. In our era, Abraham Heschel has claimed that they were who they were: prophets of God who saw what they saw, standing on their feet, with their eyes open, saying what they were told. I knew I wasn't a prophet, since what I had seen was the past, not the future. And I also knew I was not prepared to say if God and the Devil existed in some fashion. But I knew what I had seen and continued to see with my eyes. I knew that if there had been cameras to record the middle passage of the slave ships, or to record Catherine de Medici's St. Bartholomew's Day Massacre, or the campaigns of Genghis Khan, the images would have been just as horrific. But there were no cameras then. It was as if they were invented just for us, so that at our leisure we could review our own handiwork. And not just review it but *see* it with our goddamn eyes. Without the camera, I could never have seen what I saw and lived to tell of it. I could never have seen Dachau, Buchenwald, Bergen Belsen, and come out alive.

And so, for five days, I looked at the pictures and read the Bible. Every night, when I returned to the empty house where I stayed, I put my head an inch away from the speakers, turned the volume up to its limit, and played a song called "All Along the Watchtower," which Bob Dylan had written after he'd had a bad accident. One evening, just as the sun was going down, I walked along a sidewalk made of old bricks—as beautiful a yellow as I had ever seen in my life. I walked past a black man who was watching his two kids play in the yard. And I thought how pointlessly stupid racism was, since the only thing that mattered was to live. And then I went home, picked up the phone, and called every woman I'd ever loved.

Even if photographic research and the states of mind it engenders are understood, there remain other questions, such as: If photographs constitute a form of historical data, then what in fact do they reveal? With what criteria were they originally made? And with what criteria have they been selected, edited, and sequenced to form the visual essays that comprise this book?

The images, arranged in sequence, in this book form a composite portrait of the United States from 1860 to 1945, similar to a detailed photo map made of the earth's terrain by a satellite circling a hundred miles above the planet's surface. Just as no land mass can be recorded in detail in a single exposure, by a single camera, on a single pass, so no historical event can be conveyed using a single image by a single photographer, no matter how eloquent or compelling that photographer's visual language. The photographs in this book record consequences; they display mortal predicaments and trace them through time, but they do not convey causes. Thus, a photograph of the face of a frightened Marine crouching on the beach of a Pacific island does not explain how and why he came to be there. It records his mortal terror but makes no reference to Japan's East Asian Co-Prosperity Sphere nor to America's Open Door Policy. The photograph elicits projections from those who look into the Marine's eyes and imagine themselves in his place, but it does not inform them of the long-term consequences of the Russo-Japanese War, nor does it allude to the relationship between Japan's invasion of China, Roosevelt's decision to embargo American oil, and Japan's pre-emptive strike against the American fleet.

Just as the photographs in this book cannot, by themselves, delineate cause, they also cannot serve as unambiguous forms of evidence. For example, the photographs taken during the twenties of robust master farmers holding bumper crops grown in fertilized fields were made at a time when farm commodity prices were severely depressed as a result of surpluses caused by Europe's renewed ability to feed itself after the First War, as well as by the development of synthetic fibers, a change in American diet from starches to proteins, and a labor surplus caused by increased mechanization. The prosperous "modern" farmers and their wives photographed by the Agricultural Extension Service of the U.S. Department of Agriculture, were not only exceptions but were being used as models for a policy whose ultimate beneficiaries were not independent family farmers but commercial agribusiness interests that employed tenants on vast acreages.

There were similar hidden agendas in the photographs made by the Farm Security Administration (FSA) during the Depression. The FSA was the last of three federal agencies that, from 1933 to 1937, failed to do anything but spend money to alleviate the sufferings of small farmers and displaced industrial workers. The earliest of these three agencies—the Federal Emergency Relief Administration (FERA) and the Subsistence Homestead Division of the Department of the Interior—had pursued programs of emergency relief, largesse, resettlement, town planning, and the purchase and retirement of marginal farm land. By 1935, these programs were in such disarray that Roosevelt and his advisors feared they might discredit the whole administration and cost them the 1936 election. Criticism of the farm and resettlement programs had come from every direction: The American Farm Bureau—once it had convinced the administration to establish parity—criticized emergency farm relief as a communist-inspired dole that would destroy the American character; the National Association of Manufacturers claimed that industrial relocation and resettlement were expensive, socialist experiments; in the press and on the radio, Father Coughlin and Dr. Townsend made accusations of incompetency and corruption; and in the Senate, Huey Long had begun to make a case against the administration's simple inability to do anything more about the Depression than plant some trees. Meanwhile, millions of men, women, and children had become homeless wanderers. In the South, because of new acreage and crop restrictions designed to reduce farm production as part of the parity price supports of the Agricultural Adjustment Act, landlords had evicted 100,000 tenants from land that had been withdrawn from cultivation. In the West, the soil of Oklahoma, Arkansas, Montana, and South Dakota had turned to dust and blown whole counties to California.

In 1935, the Resettlement Administration (RA)—the second one of the agencies to precede the Farm Security Administration—was formed as a flanking and counterattack that would silence Roosevelt's political opponents and convince the American people that the president deserved another term. The director of this new agency was a former Columbia University economics professor named Tugwell, who hired one of his old instructors, a man named Stryker, who then hired such luminous photographers as Walker Evans, Dorothea Lange, Russell Lee, and Arthur Rothstein to make pictures of rural poverty the administration could then use in news releases, exhibitions, and films to convince the American people that their government was both compassionate and competent. The results of this effort were somewhat mixed: By June 1936, the RA had spent $95 million helping two million farm people stay where they were; by the end of the year, Roosevelt had been re-elected, but Tugwell had been forced to resign. And, by 1937, Walker Evans, who was an artist, quit and was fired by Stryker, who was a company man.

There are two reasons for reciting such hidden agendas: First, a knowledge of historical context is as useful when looking at photographs in books as it is when searching for them in archive; second, although such knowledge is useful, it is not enough. The fact is that photographers make images not only to satisfy their employers but also to please themselves. Whatever the agendas of the organizations that use their images—whether those organizations are government agencies, postcard publishers, or galleries—photographers have their own definitions of utility and excellence. Dorothea Lange, Walker Evans, and Ben Shahn were thinking and seeing long before and long after Stryker hired them as civil servant contract employees.

There are many photographers who do what they're told and earn their living by making photographs that resemble other photographs. But there are others who see what no one else has seen, and make images that have the surprising inevitability of true inventions. Such photographers resemble hunters, collectors, and gamblers. What they gamble with and count on is something Jung called synchroneous, or meaningful, coincidences, and what they hunt and collect are the entities Goethe called archetypal phenomena. Goethe believed that all natural phenomena exist in a continuous series of increasing complexity. "Goethe calls the simplest cases that show a phenomenon with the greatest possible clarity and from which other phenomena may be derived *Urphenomene*. . . . Nothing lies beyond these archetypal phenomena [which] represent the ultimate range of perception attainable to us." [Rudolph Magnus, *Goethe as a Scientist*, translated by Heinz Norden (New York: Henry Shuman, 1949), p. 225.] Thus, Goethe believed that the archetypal phenomenon of geology was granite, a rock whose structure was so basic and so immediately obvious to perception that its significance and its appearance coincided. This idea of correspondence between appearance and significance, between outer and inner nature, was enunciated again and again by James Agee in *Let Us Now Praise Famous Men*. But he said it no more clearly than in the introduction to *Many Are Called* (New York: Houghton Mifflin, 1966), a collection of portraits made by Walker Evans on the New York subways: "Those who use the subways are several millions, they are members of every race and every nation of the earth, they are of all ages, of all temperaments, of all classes, of almost every imaginable occupation. . . . Each . . . is an individual existence as matchless as a thumbprint or a snowflake. Each wears garments which, of themselves, are exquisitely subtle uniforms and badges of their being. And each carries, in the postures of his body, in his hands, in his face, in the eyes, the signatures of a time and a place in the world. . . . The simplest or the strongest of these beings has been so designed upon by his existence that he has a wound and nakedness to conceal, and guards and disguises by which he conceals it. Scarcely ever, in the whole of his living, are these guards down. Before every other human being, in no matter what intimate trust, in no matter what apathy, something of the mask is there. . . . Only in sleep, and not fully there, or only in certain waking moments of suspension, of quiet, of solitude, are those guards down, and these moments are only rarely to be seen by the person himself or by any other human being." Because of their alertness, and because of their restless journeys into the world, these other human beings are often photographers. They are the ones who seek to penetrate the masks of people and to master the language of things. The few photographers who actually master this language are the spiritual descendants of Dürer, who, said Erasmus, "even depicts what cannot be depicted: fire, rays of light, thunderstorms, sheet lightning, or even, as the saying goes, the clouds upon the wall; all the characters and emotions; in fine, the whole mind of man as it shines forth from the body, and almost the very voice" [*Symbols in Transformation* (Princeton, NJ: Princeton Art Museum, 1969), p. 16.] Those few photographers who understand this correspondence between outer and inner state read the world as if it were an allegory and pass through it as if they were pilgrims on a journey, looking for signs. It is because of their alertness to such signs, to the ways in which form manifests content, that their images of the world are as revealing as the most precise and cogent written data. It is because of, rather than in spite of, their knowledge of appearances that their photographs reveal the tacit assumptions of a place and a people in time.

Such photographers also share an understanding of the kind of luck known to gamblers and hunters. It is luck, based on desire, that takes the form of being in the right place at the right time. Carl Jung observed such coincidences in his practice for thirty years. One of the most striking occurred during the treatment of a well-educated and very rational young woman who used her reason to deflect whatever insights her therapy might have offered her. "After several fruitless attempts to sweeten her rationalism with a somewhat more human understanding, I had to confine myself [writes Jung] to the hope that something . . . would burst the intellectual retort in which she had sealed herself. . . . I was sitting opposite her one day with my back to the window, listening to her. . . . She had had an impressive dream the night before in which someone had given her a golden scarab. . . . While she was telling me this dream, I heard something behind me, gently tapping on the window. I turned round and saw that it was a fairly large flying insect that was knocking against the windowpane. . . . This seemed to me very strange. I opened the window immediately and caught the insect in the air as it flew in. It was a Scarabaeid beetle, or common rose-chafer . . . whose golden green color most nearly resembles that of a golden scarab. I handed the beetle to my patient with the words, 'Here is your scarab.' This experience punctured the desired hole in her rationalism and broke the ice of her intellectual resistance." [Carl Jung, *The Structure and Dynamics of the Psyche*, Collected Works,

vol. 8, translated by R. F. C. Hull, Bollingen Series XX (Princeton, NJ: Princeton University Press, 1969), pp. 525–26.]

Jung defined such coincidences as "the simultaneous occurrence of a certain psychic state [in this example, the intense desire of a therapist for a sign that defied rational explanation] with one or more external events which appear as meaningful parallels to the momentary subjective state. . . ." (*Ibid*, p. 441.) Jung believed such coincidences were composed of "two factors: (a) an unconscious image comes into consciousness either directly (i.e., literally) or indirectly (symbolized or suggested) in the form of a dream, idea, or premonition; (b) an objective situation coincides with this content." (*Ibid*, p. 447.) If the principal subject is not a therapist but a photographer, and if the objective situation is not a study but a street, then instead of opening a window and capturing an insect, which is the literal reproduction of a dream image, the photographer takes a picture of an event he somehow recognizes only because he has already glimpsed it, without fully knowing it, in his mind's eye.

Jung emphasizes the role that desire plays in such occurrences. He quotes Albertus Magnus, a fifteenth-century alchemist, who alludes to a work of magic "'which says that a certain power to alter things indwells in the human soul and subordinates the other things to her, particularly when she is swept into a great excess of love, hate, or the like.'" (Albertus Magnus, *De mirabilibus mundi*, *Ibid*, p. 448.) Thus, hunters driven by hunger, gamblers by avarice, and photographers by entrancement and curiosity—all participate in a subtle interaction with the world, which draws them outward as they draw it in, making their moves in middle breath. The great ones, the ones of heart and stamina, do what they do, find what they seek again and again, not only because they have mastered their craft but also because, like a starving man who finds a quarter on a street, they dwell constantly on their desire.

It is this very attentiveness to their own preoccupations, combined with an unusual alertness to the meaning of appearances, that places the more remarkable of photographers at an intersection of events that are both beyond their control and of their own making. The images they create are the result not only of their mastery of composition but also of a soundless and momentary collision between what they hope and fear they are and what the world is and pretends to be. The marks of such collisions were the criteria used to select the images in this book. Not all of the photographs you will see bear these marks, but many of them do, and many others show evidence of close calls and near misses.

Books of photographs, no matter how carefully crafted their sequences, are often caught in conventions that alter their intent: Nearly everyone browses through them from back to front or from middle to end, and almost no one has the initial patience to read their introductory prose before stealing a glance at their images. What the author intended as a coda becomes an inadvertent preface; what he intended as a bridge becomes a summary; what he intended as an uninterrupted series is broken by the ring of a phone or the cry of a child. Even if a book of photographs is perused from its front to its back, the burden of meaning is still placed on the mind and imagination of its "reader" since, in spite of the book's inherent visual architecture, its "text" is mute, drawing its motive power from both the implicitness of art and the explicitness of scholarship. At its best, a book of photographs is the equivalent of a machine without moving parts, activated by the imagination of its viewer, a perpetual motion device geared without friction, lubricated by its very use, capable of generating enough energy to light a room, a house, an entire district, perhaps a whole city.

What you are holding in your hands is the twentieth-century equivalent of a book of emblems, the first collection of which, entitled *Emblemata*, was published in 1531 by Alciati for the intellectual and moral edification of gentlemen and ladies of learning. The emblems collected by Alciati were composed of three elements: a recognizable but somewhat puzzling image, often an allegorical cliché or visual commonplace (such as a female nude that might be understood as a symbol of vanity as well as an allusion to Venus or Bathsheba); a title or motto that clarified some of the ambiguity of the image; and an allusive commentary that celebrated the moral, aesthetic, philosophical, or political speculations that the image and its motto had provoked. The emblem's image began these speculations and reinforced them as the viewer/reader glanced from image to motto to text and back again, using visual clues to decipher the text's allusions and using written evidence to clarify the image's ambiguities. In this way, the emblem's interplay of image, title, and text caused the viewer/reader to see something first as itself, then as the embodiment of an idea, and then as part of a conceptual pattern. The documentary photographs in this book serve the same function: They are sufficiently recognizable but also sufficiently puzzling to engage your attention and imagination; they provoke a limited range of associative thoughts and projections that can be clarified by the captions that accompany them; and they intellectually and emotionally engage you to search for clarification either from other written sources, or from this introduction, or from the preface that accompanies it, or from the other images that, in sequence, form the text of the book. If the machinery of this book works even once as it was intended, your idle glance will become a look, your look a gaze, your gaze a thought, and your thought the first of many about how this country came to inhabit its place in time.

Bearing Witness

1/"A lone grave on the battlefield of Antietam." Brady's Album Gallery.

The
Civil War

2/Bv't Major General William T. Clark.

3/Captain Theron E. Hall, A.S.M. Acquina Creek, Virginia. February 1863.

4/Colonel William D. Mann,
7th Michigan Cavalry.

5/Captain Cunningham. Beaton, Virginia. August 1863.

6/Union cavalry officer.

7/Brigadier General C. C. Dodge,
Union Army.

9/Bv't. Major General Daniel C.
McCallum.

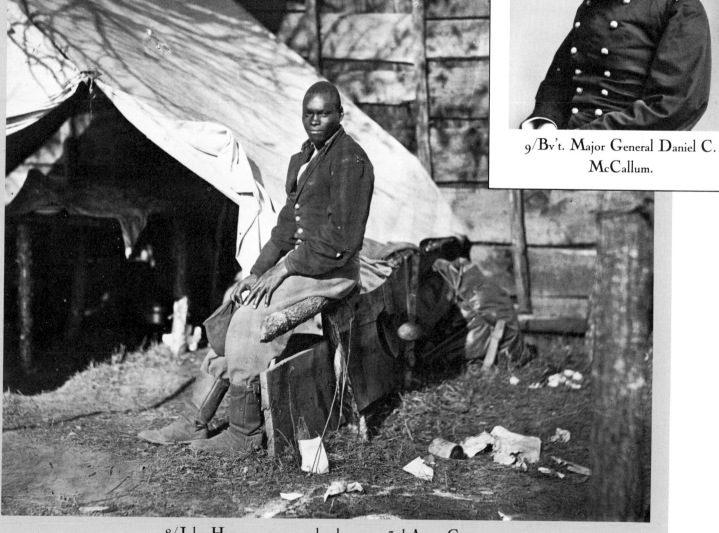

8/John Henry, a servant at headquarters, 3rd Army Corps.

10/Soldier group.

11/Atlanta, Georgia.

6

12/General Caldwell and staff on battlefield of Antietam. September 21, 1862.

13/Falmouth, Virginia.

14/"A relic of Pope's retreat."

15/Federal soldier disemboweled by a shell. Gettysburg, Pennsylvania.

16/Atlanta, Georgia.

17/"Confederate horse killed at Antietam." Brady's Album Gallery.

The
West

1/Iceberg Canyon, Colorado River. 1871.

2/The great hostile camp. Deadwood, South Dakota. 1891.

12

3/"Spotted Horse." May 24, 1900.

4/"Clear." May 24, 1900.

5/Navaho dancer.

6/Navaho dancer.

7/Navaho dancer.

8/"Indian chiefs who counciled with General Miles and settled the Indian war: (*seated, left to right*) Standing Bull,
Bear Who Looks Back Running, Has the Big White Horse, White Tail, and Liver Bear; (*standing, left to right*) Little Thunder, Bull Dog,
High Hawk, Lame, and Eagle Pipe. Deadwood, South Dakota. 1891."

9/"The cavalier. The young soldier and his horse on duty at Camp Cheyenne. 1890."

10/"Roping gray wolf—cowboys take in a gray wolf on 'round-up' in Wyoming. 1887."

11/"Wells Fargo Express Company treasure wagon and guards with $250,000 in gold bullion from the Great Homestake Mine. Deadwood, South Dakota. 1890."

12/"'We have it rich'—Old-timers Spriggs, Lamb, and Dillon at work washing and panning gold. Rockerville, South Dakota. 1889."

13/From Forrest Hill. Deadwood, South Dakota. 1888.

14/"Mills and mines, part of the Great Homestake works.
Lead City, South Dakota. 1889."

15/"Indian chiefs and U.S. officials: [*positions n.a.*] Two Strike, Crow Dog, Short Bull, High Hawk, Two Lance, Kicking Bear, Good Voice, Thunder Hawk, Rocky Bear, Young Man Afraid of His Horse, American Horse, W. F. (Buffalo Bill) Cody, Major J. M. Burk, J. C. Craiger, J. McDonald, and J. G. Worth. Pine Ridge, South Dakota. January 16, 1891."

16/Buffalo Bill Cody

Black Life

1/Students at Miss Davis's School at the Russell Farm of the Thompson Plantation. Ca. 1903.

2/Mother and children. Hampton, Virginia.

3/"Seventy summers in the cotton fields." 1899.

4/"We's done all dis s'mornin." 1899.

5/A Mississippi River landing. Memphis, Tennessee. 1906.

6/"Sally in our alley." 1897.

7/"Romeo and Juliet."

8/Woman seated. Tuskegee Institute. 1906.

9/Young woman at Tuskegee Institute. Alabama. 1906.

10/Charles Chestnut. Tuskegee Institute. 1906.

11/Booker T. Washington. Tuskegee Institute. 1906.

12/George Washington Carver. Tuskegee Institute. 1906.

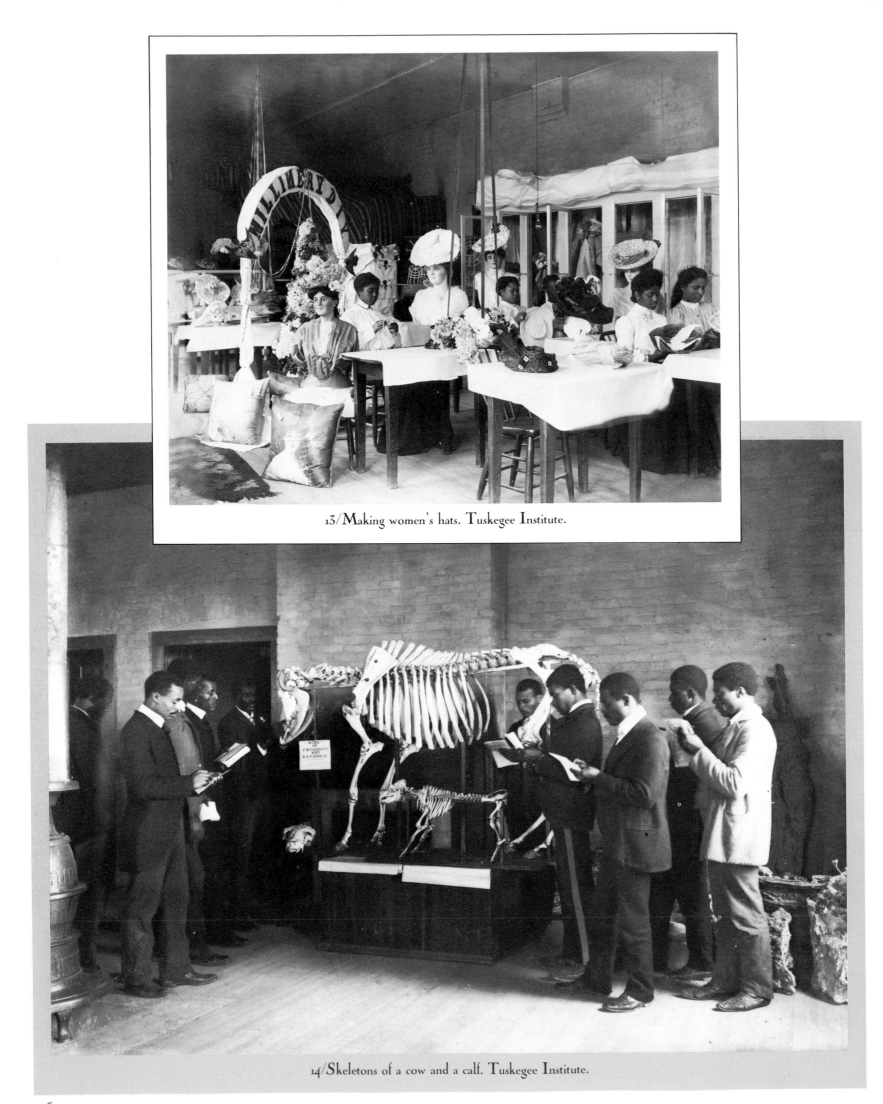

13/Making women's hats. Tuskegee Institute.

14/Skeletons of a cow and a calf. Tuskegee Institute.

15/History class. Tuskegee Institute.

16/Tuskegee Institute. Ca. 1902.

17/Tuskegee Institute. Ca. 1902.

18/Pledging allegiance. Hampton, Virginia.

City
Life

1/Manhattan Bridge under construction. New York, New York.

2/Brooklyn terminal, Brooklyn Bridge. New York, New York. 1903.

3/"Harp and Fiddle." Chicago, Illinois. 1891.

4/"A musical family."

5/Gas company employee. Chicago, Illinois. 1891.

6/Coal peddler. Chicago, Illinois. 1891.

7/Street sweeper. Chicago, Illinois. 1891.

8/Berry peddler. Chicago, Illinois. 1891.

9/Flatiron Building. New York, New York. 1903.

10/Board of Trade session. Chicago, Illinois. 1905.

11/Tenement. New York, New York. 1905.

12/People sitting outside at night during hot weather. New York, New York.

13/"Actress at home." New York, New York.

14/"Toledo Beach from Chutes."

15/Teddy Roosevelt's son, Kermit, and his dog, Jack.

16/Urchin. Ca. 1890.

17/"Billboards hiding a garbage dump." Suburban Boston. Ca. 1890.

Industry
and
Agriculture

1/Carnegie furnaces. Braddock, Pennsylvania. 1905.

2/Quincy mine, shaft number 2. Hancock, Michigan. 1906.

3/Casting pig iron. Iroquois smelter. Chicago, Illinois.

4/Pouring copper. Hancock, Michigan. 1906.

5/Woodward coal breakers. Kingston, Pennsylvania. 1900.

6/"Finishing (sandpapering) automobile wheels." Detroit, Michigan.

7/"Experts testing engines in an automobile plant." Detroit, Michigan.

8/National Cash Register Company. Dayton, Ohio. 1902.

9/"Beaming frames where threads are straightened for looms." White Oak Mills. Greensboro, North Carolina. 1907.

10/"Blowing the bottle into required shape in a mould. American Glass Bottle Industry." 1907.

11/"Quarrying granite—drilling preparatory to splitting." Concord, New Hampshire. 1903.

12/"Emptying the kiln." St. Louis, Missouri.

13/"Removing from the furnace the crucibles full of fiery liquid bronze." John Williams Foundry. New York. 1904.

14/Open pit mine. Duluth, Minnesota. 1906.

15/American Steel & Wire Co. 1901.

16/Ore dock. Two Harbors, Minnesota.

17/"Loading a king hoist in hold—showing pickmen at work." Conneaut, Ohio. 1905.

18/"Hydraulic ore-unloaders that lift 1,800 tons an hour, and laden lake vessel." Cleveland, Ohio. 1906.

19/Unloading ore from whaleback. Buffalo, New York.

20/Steelworks. Homestead, Pennsylvania.

21/"How drinking water is furnished to 8,000 men—
water boys going to refill their pails." Steelworks.
Homestead, Pennsylvania. 1907.

22/Loading scrap. Steelworks. Homestead, Pennsylvania. 1908.

23/"Cleaning and repairing ladle—view showing method of lining." Steelworks. Pittsburgh, Pennsylvania.

24/Red Jacket mine shaft. Calumet, Michigan. 1906.

25/Agricultural machinery. Kansas. 1911.

26/Cotton mill workers.

27/"Record load of wheat." 1909.

28/Apple picking. Berkeley Company.
West Virginia. 1910.

29/"The undefeated." 1906.

1/Striker moving toward camera. Bayonne, New Jersey. July 1915.

Child Labor
and
Strikes

2/Mill boys.

3/Cannery girl sitting with her sister.

4/Mill boy.

5/Young tobacco picker.

6/Injured mill boy.

7/Mill workers.

8/Coal miners.

9/Massachusetts militia guarding approach to mills. Lawrence, Massachusetts. January 1912.

10/"Police with battered striker, Philadelphia streetcar strike." 1910.

11/"Colt gun on auto—used during streetcar strike." Columbus, Ohio. July 1910.

12/"Casualties of anarchist bombing. Union Square, New York, twenty seconds after bomb explosion."
March 30, 1908.

The Philippine Insurrection

1/Spanish shells, Cavite arsenal, Philippines.

2/American troops defending a street barricade.

3/American troops resting behind a paddy dike.

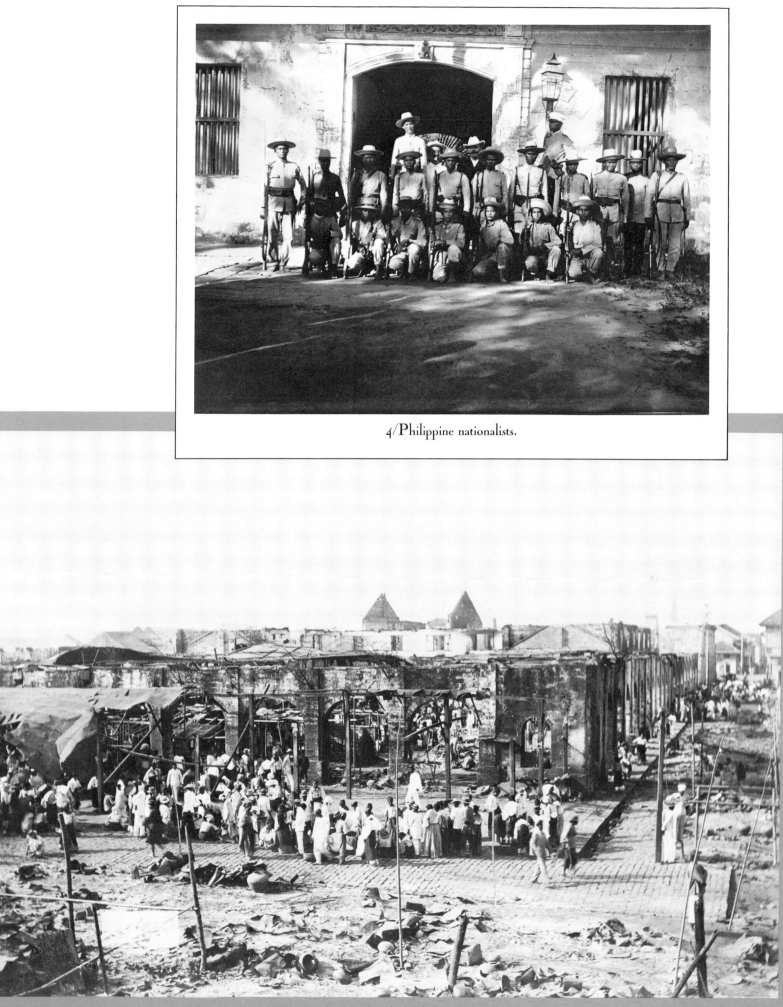

4/Philippine nationalists.

5/Ruins of an unidentified Philippine town.

6/American riflemen firing a volley.

7/American officers.

8/"In front of the Kansas line near Caloocan."

9/"Father and son."

10/"A few captured at Pasay and Paranque."

11/"Filipino prisoners of war." Cavite, Philippines.

12/U.S.–Philippine Commission. *Second from right:* Admiral Dewey. *Third from right:* General MacArthur.

13/U.S. Army Signal Corps personnel and their servants.

Ideal
and
Comic
Types

1/Dancers of Isadora Duncan.

2/J. D. Hoffman, baseball player. Philadelphia, Pennsylvania. American League, 1903–1909.

3/"Ray Bronson, America's premier lightweight."

4/"The boys of the LS Ranch near Tascosa, Texas, lingering at the chuckwagon after the day's work is done, listening to the stories of Linger, range boss of the LS." 1908.

5/Marine officer. 1900.

6/"Secondhand Rose."

7/"Sisters." 1902.

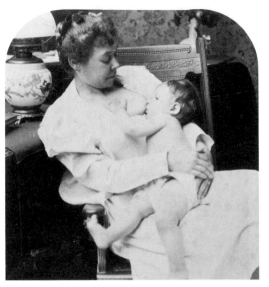

8/"Baby's happy hour."

9/Mrs. Moore.

10/"Now ride the goat, and do it pretty." 1902.

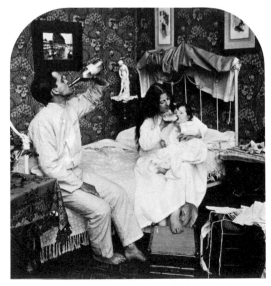

11/"A chip off the old block." 1906.

12/"The good story."

13/The new woman—washday. 1901.

14/Ethel Reed, poster artist.

15/"Diagnosing the case of Miss Love." 1905.

16/"The doctor applies a simple remedy." 1905.

17/"'Alone! At Last, Alone!' Hero in love and war."

Misfortunes

1/"Johnstown flood—Lost 10,000–12,000 lives. May 31, 1889."

2/San Francisco earthquake.

3/"The Johnstown calamity—a slightly
damaged house."

4/San Francisco earthquake. May 1906.

5/San Francisco earthquake—cremating the dead.

6/"The hanging of Loris Higgins."
Bancroft, Nebraska. 1807.

7/"City Hall, San Francisco earthquake." May 1906.

World
War
One

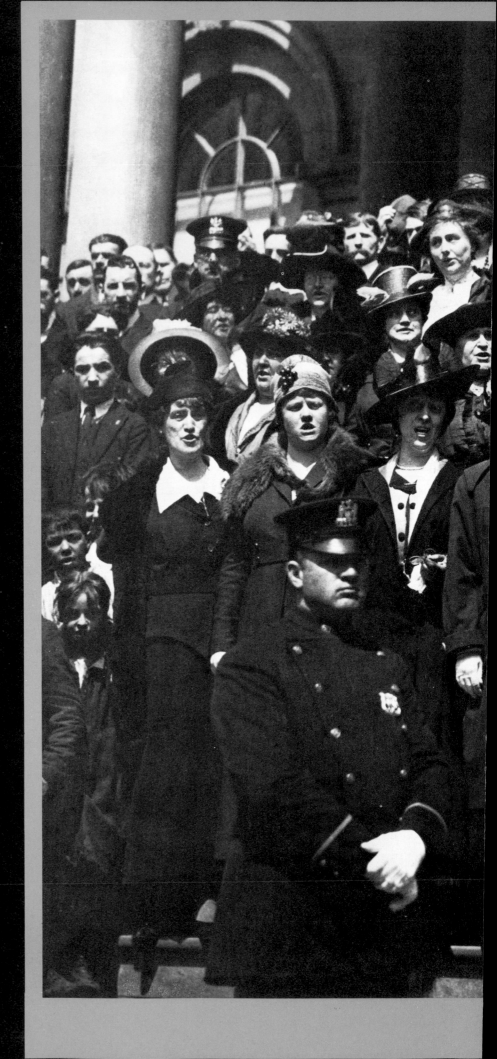

1/"Liberty Loan Choir sings on the steps of City Hall, New York City, during third Liberty Loan campaign.
Bishop William Wilkinson leads the choir. April 1918."

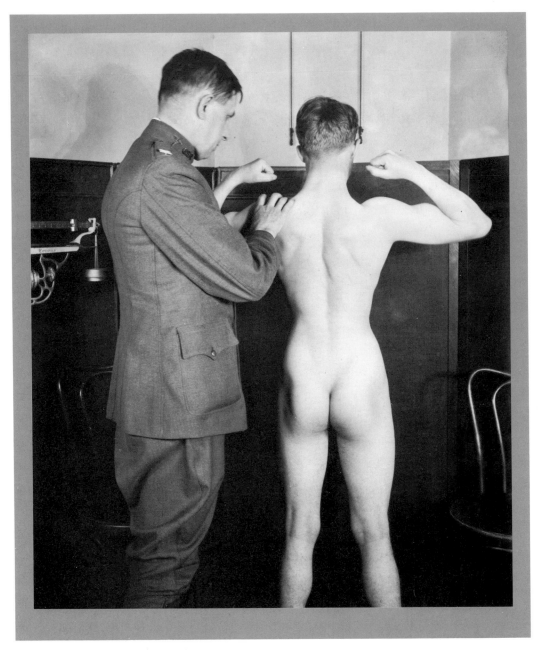

2/"Physical examination of an aviation recruit.
Episcopal Hospital,
Washington, D.C. April 1918."

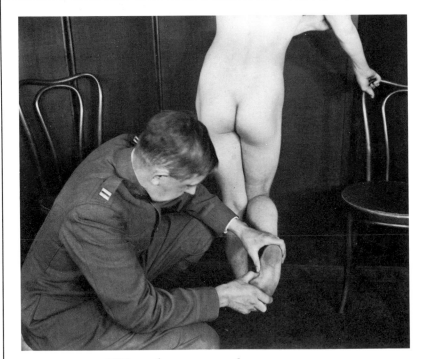

3/"Physical examination of aviation recruit—
checking for flat feet. April 1918."

4/"Physical examination of aviation recruit—
checking for hemorrhoids. April 1918."

5/"Outfitting recruits at Camp Meade,
Maryland. Each recruit is issued a clothing slip,
which is then stamped with a number.
October 4, 1918."

6/"Outfitting recruits, Camp Meade, Maryland. Each recruit is measured.
Results are marked on his clothing slip. October 1918."

7/"General John J. Pershing at his desk." France.

9/"American defensive grenade, fragmented exterior."

10/"Incendiary bomb. February 1918."

8/"A view of the ruins of Arocourt. October 6, 1918."

11/"General William H. Johnston observing the progress of battle. Hill 274, near Mt. Des Allieaux, France, 3:40 A.M. September 26, 1918."

12/"An American patrol displays a machine gun it captured without firing a shot.
The patrol captured the German weapon and its crew in the St. Mihiel salient, while the Germans were off-guard."

13/"View of the dugouts of the 79th Division at Vacherauville, Meuse, north of Verdun. October 1918."

14/"Troops of U.S. 317-319th Ambulance Company's 305th sanitary train, singing in church at Vaux, Ardennes, France. November 5, 1918."

15/"Treatment room for troops who've been gassed."

16/"Shower bath, 166th Field Hospital, Baccarat, France.
May 16, 1918."

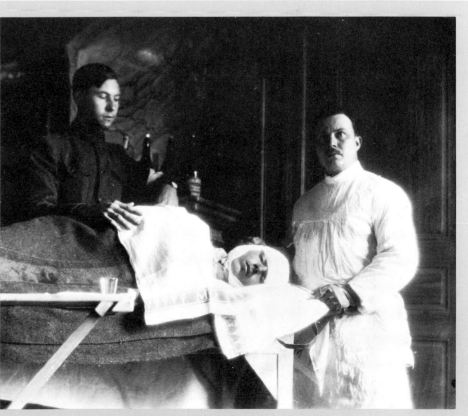

17/"American base hospital, France."

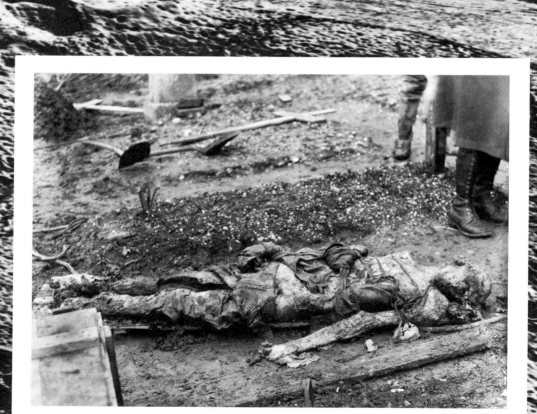

19/"Body of Captain Blanton Barrett, buried by Germans on July 22,
Neurthe-et-Moselle, France. A card found in a pocket announced the birth of a daughter,
named Caroline, to Captain and Mrs. Barrett. Card was used to identify
the corpse. April 3, 1919."

18/"Mine craters. Combres Hill, France."

Women after the War

1/"Women rivet heaters and passers on ship construction work. Navy yard, Puget Sound, Washington. May 1919."

2/"The Cleveland Hardware Company—very crowded lunchroom. April 1927."

3/"Colored lunchroom in a factory."

4/"Armour and Company, Chicago—girls and men wrapping and packing bacon. January 1919."

5/"Sweet Sixteen, #1."

6/"Syncopating Sue, #15."

7/"Hooker Electric Chemical Company, Niagara Falls, New York. Women constructing concrete forms—lighting and working conditions poor. January 1919."

8/"The Girl on the Moon, #1."

9/"Tootsie the Toe Dancer, #5."

1/"Field of black winter wheat on summer fallow ground. Fleming, Colorado. 1926."

Farm Life

2/"Farmer showing soybeans that have and have not been grown in ground treated with lime. Transylvania County, North Carolina. September 1925."

3/"Dusting cotton. Athens, Georgia. July 1929."

4/"Cabbage plants in ideal condition for shipping. Pickens County, South Carolina. November 1926."

5/"Farm woman feeding her pullets. Henry County, Ohio. August 1927."

6/"Farmer and his wife painting their front porch. Grand Traverse County, Michigan. July 1926."

7/"Farmer and his wife reading and sewing by lamplight. Laurel, Maryland. 1928."

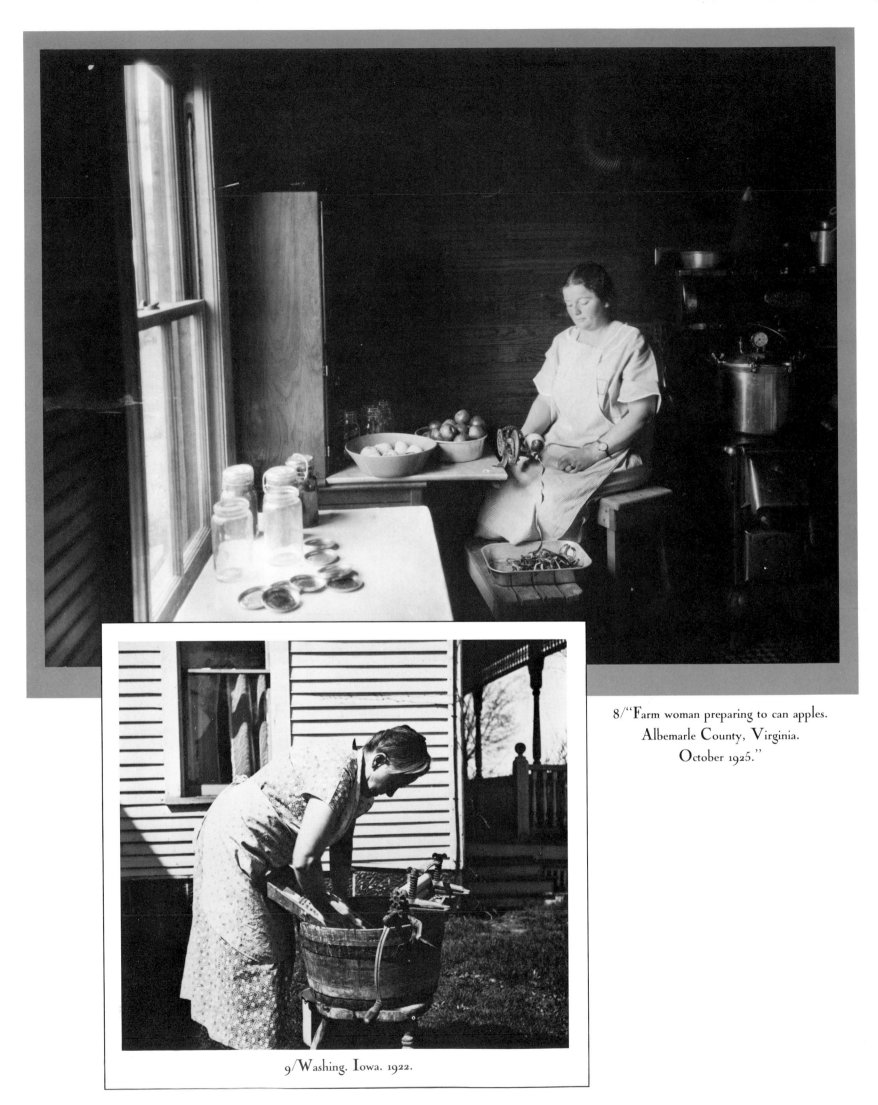

8/"Farm woman preparing to can apples. Albemarle County, Virginia. October 1925."

9/Washing. Iowa. 1922.

10/"Kitchen with wood range and no
electric light. Maryland.
April 1929."

11/Sweeping the floor. Maryland. 1929.

12/"Farmer and his family. Roanoke County, Virginia. August 1926."

13/"Master farmer and his wife. South Carolina. 1928."

The
Depression

1/"Sweetwater County, Wyoming. Highway U.S. 30. March 1940."

2/"Migratory bean-pickers. Child at end of the day in a bean-picker's camp. West Stayton, Marion County, Oregon. August 1939."

4/"A woman flood refugee in a schoolhouse. Sikeston, Missouri. January 1937."

3/(*opposite page*) and 5/"An aged cotton farmer who inherited his lands, which are heavily mortgaged now. Greene County, Georgia. July 1937."

6/"A destitute family. The Ozark Mountains area, Arkansas. October 1935."

7/"Unemployed youth. Washington, D.C. August 1938."

8/"Migrant family saying grace before their noon-day meal by the side of the road. Fort Gibson, Oklahoma. June 1939."

9/"Entrance to an apartment house in the black belt. Chicago, Illinois. April 1941."

10/"R. B. Whitley, who was one of the first citizens of the town. He is one of the leading citizens, owner of the general store, president of the bank, and owner of a cotton mill and a farm. Wendell, North Carolina. November 1939."

11/"A Negro family who live on a cotton patch. Vicksburg, Mississippi, in the Delta area. July 1936."

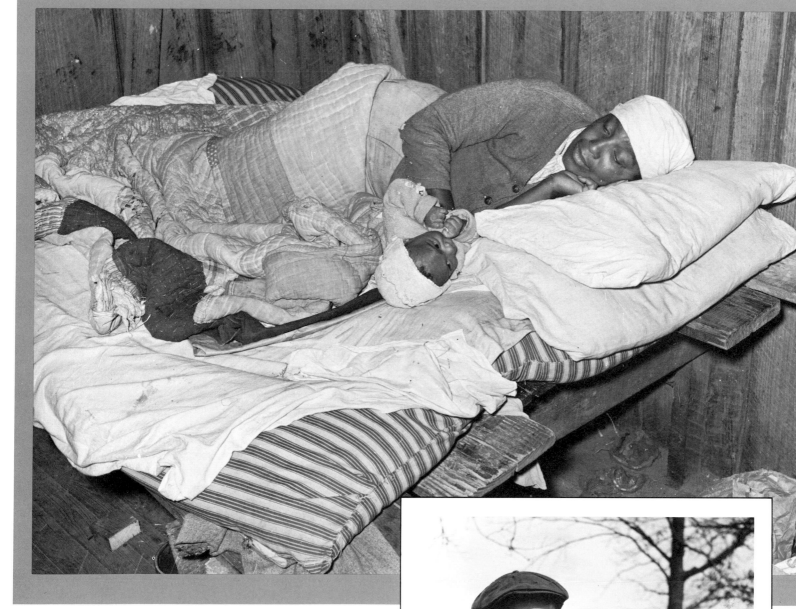

12/"A Negro mother and baby in the house furnished to them while working in the strawberry fields. Independence, Louisiana. April 1939."

13/"Evicted sharecropper and his child. New Madrid County, Missouri. January 1939."

14/"Houses and Negroes in a slum district. Atlanta, Georgia. March 1936."

15/"Negro man entering movie theater by 'Colored' entrance. Belzoni, Mississippi, in the Delta area.
October 1939."

16/"A community planned by the Suburban Division of the U.S. Resettlement Administration. Greendale, Wisconsin. September 1939."

17/"Newport News homestead, a U.S. Resettlement Administration housing project. The resident engineer (*center*) and his assistants. Newport News, Virginia. September 1936."

18/"The interior of a general store. Moundville, Alabama. 1935."

19/"Newsstand. Omaha, Nebraska. November 1938."

20/"Victory Through Christ Society holding its Sunday morning revival in a garage. Testimony: 'He's such a wonderful savior, glory to God. I'm so glad I came to him. Praise God. His love is so wonderful. He's coming soon. I want to praise the Lord for what He is to me. He saved me one time and filled me with the Holy Ghost. Hallelujah! He will fill your heart today. Bless His holy name!' Dos Palos, California. June 1938."

21/"Mildrid Irwin, entertainer, in a saloon. She entertained for twenty years in Omaha before coming to North Platte. North Platte, Nebraska. October 1938."

22/"Dancing in a roadhouse. Raceland, Louisiana. September 1938."

23/"Some men and women at Filipak's bar. Shenandoah, Pennsylvania. 1938."

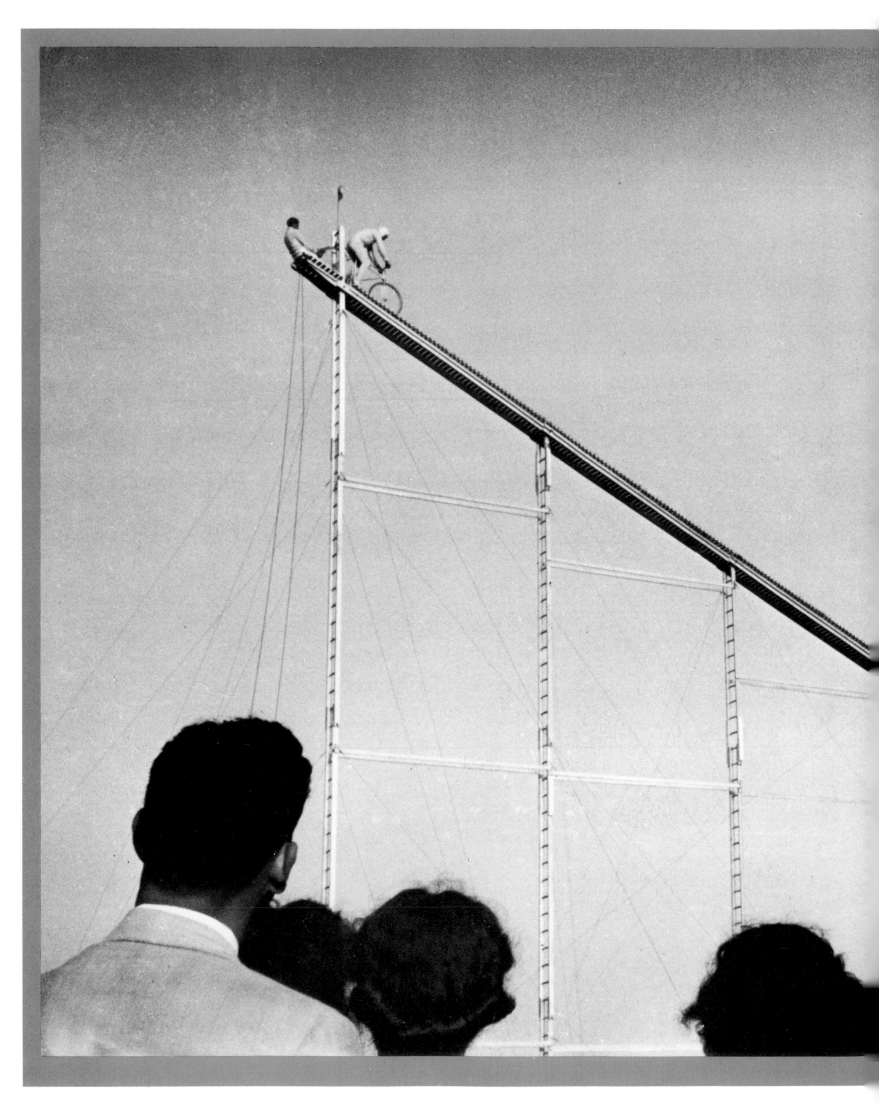

25/"Cars parked along the highway near the Duke University stadium during the football game between Duke University and the University of North Carolina. Durham, North Carolina. November 1939."

24/"A crowd watching a daredevil preparing to dive into the water on a bicycle, down an elevated incline, at the South Louisiana State Fair. Donaldsonville, Louisiana. November 1938."

1/"Ship sliding off the shipways. Bethlehem-Fairfield shipyards. Baltimore, Maryland. May 1943."

2/"Workman reading a war extra. Shasta Dam, Shasta County, California. December 1941."

War
Mobilization

3/"Street corner. Bismarck, North Dakota. March 1943."

4/"Line at a rationing board. New Orleans, Louisiana.
March 1943."

5/"Thousands of skilled craftsmen all over America enter the gates of warplane factories each day. Employees must display their badges and identification cards before admittance. North American Aviation, Inc. Inglewood, California. 1942."

6/"Election of officers to Ford Local 600, United Automobile Workers, Congress of Industrial Organizations—80,000 River Rouge Ford plant workers voted. Detroit, Michigan. April 1942."

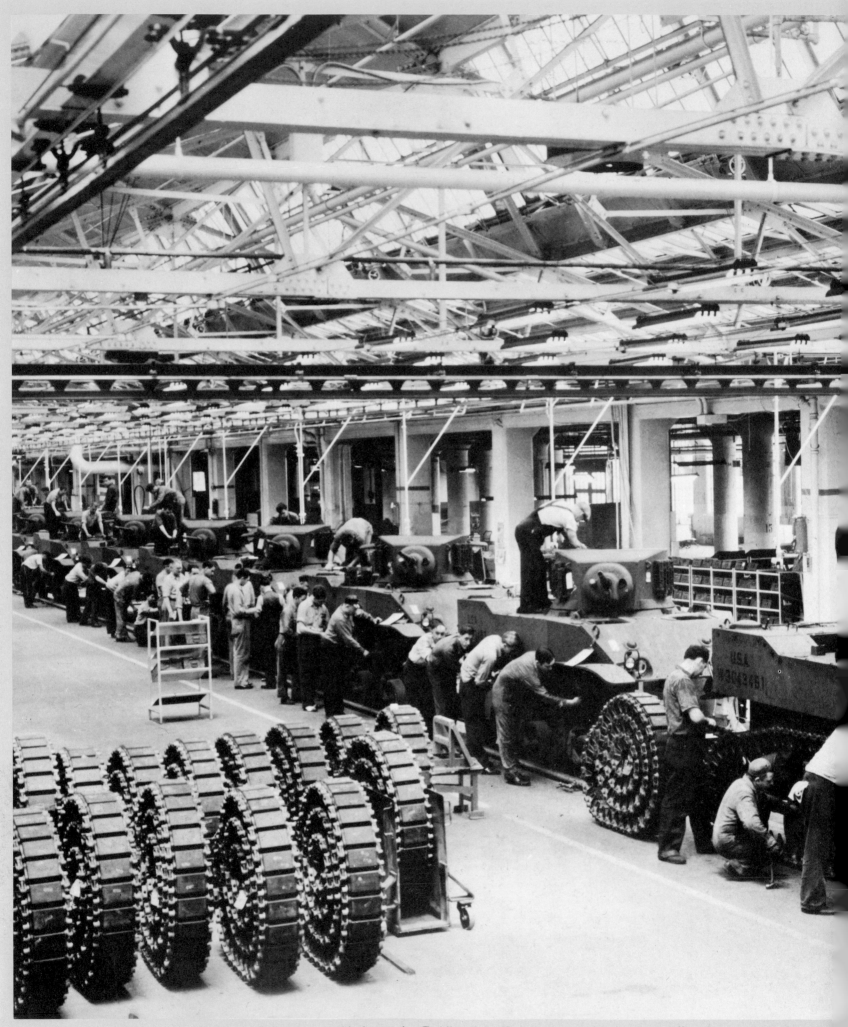

7/ "M-5 tanks on the assembly line at the Cadillac plant. Detroit vicinity, Michigan. 1942."

8/Assembly line where B-25 bombers are rapidly being built. North American Aviation, Inc. Inglewood, California 1942."

9/Air Service Command. Early morning mass calisthenics. Daniel Field, Georgia. July 1943.

Workers
and
Citizens

1/"Welder at the Higgins shipyards. New Orleans, Louisiana. June 1943."

2/"Woman arc welder. Bethlehem-Fairfield shipyards. Baltimore, Maryland. May 1943."

3/"Member of the U.S. Rural Electrification Administration Cooperative. Hayti, Missouri. July 1942."

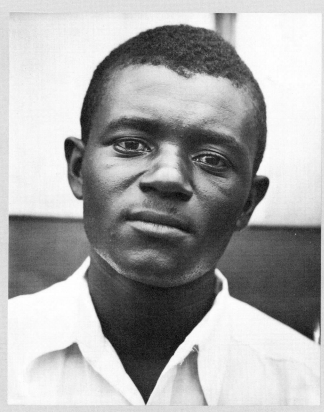

4/"Councilman—Farm Security Administration agricultural workers' camp. Bridgeton, New Jersey. June 1942."

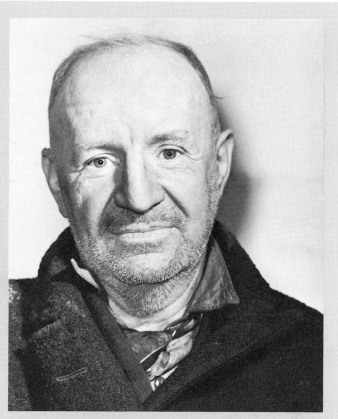

5/"Merchant seaman. New York, New York. December 1941."

6/"Trainman with a cigar. Bethlehem-Fairfield shipyards. Baltimore, Maryland. May 1943."

7/"Welder's helper. Douglas Dam, Tennessee. (Tennessee Valley Authority.) June 1942."

8/"Steelworker, president of the Serbian Club. Aliquippa, Pennsylvania. January 1941."

9/"Mr. T. J. Long, a railroad operator and farmer, who is president of the farmers' tri-county cooperative market. Du Bois, Pennsylvania. August 1940."

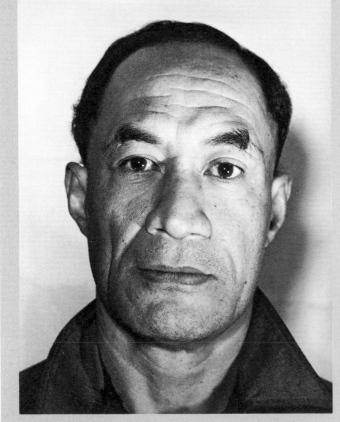

10/"Merchant seaman. New York, New York. December 1941."

11/"A member of the county agricultural council. Ross County, Ohio. February 1940."

12/"Overseer of the grange. Fairfax County, Virginia. January 1940."

13/"The Central Iowa 4-H Club Fair—a 4-H Club boy. Marshalltown, Iowa. February 1940."

14/"An officer of the United Mine Workers of America. Herrin, Illinois. January 1939."

15/"Merchant seaman. New York, New York. December 1941."

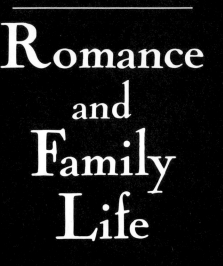

Romance
and
Family
Life

1 and 2/"Laura and Frank Czaya, a couple of Polish descent, in the living room of the home they share with Laura's mother, aunt, and brother in Depew. Frank is home on a ten-day furlough. Laura works in the nearby Symington-Gould plant. Buffalo, New York. May 1943."

3/"Mr. and Mrs. Dyson, an aged couple who have received an FSA rehabilitation loan. St. Mary's County, Maryland. September 1940."

4/"Farm Security Administration borrowers. Grant County, Illinois. May 1940."

5/"Mr. Westerberg inspecting Mrs. Westerberg's dinner preparation of Swedish dishes. The Westerbergs came from Eskilstuna, Sweden, in 1924. Cass Lake, near Pontiac, Michigan. September 1942."

6/"The Farm Security Administration's camp for migratory workers. Harlingen, Texas. February 1942."

7/"Guests of a trailer park. Sarasota, Florida. January 1941."

8/"Kenneth C. Hall and family in the living room of their home on a defense housing project. Sheffield, Alabama. (Tennessee Valley Authority.) June 1942."

9/A community settled by about 200 migrant Texas and Oklahoma farmers who filled homestead claims. Round dance. Among people where square dancing is the usual form of dance, regular ballroom dancing is called "round dancing." Pie Town, New Mexico. June 1940.

10/Jitterbugs at an Elks Club dance, the "cleanest dance in town." Washington, D.C. April 1943.

11/"Girl sitting alone in the *Sea Grill*, a bar and restaurant, waiting for a pickup. 'I come in here pretty often, sometimes alone, mostly with another girl. We drink beer, and talk, and of course we keep our eyes open. You'd be surprised how often nice, lonesome, soldiers ask *S*ue, the waitress, to introduce them to us.' Washington, D.C. April 1943."

12/"Mrs. Ella Watson, a government charwoman, with three grandchildren and her adopted daughter. Washington, D.C. August 1942."

13/"A mountain woman and her grandchild sitting on the porch of their home in Frozen Creek, Breathitt County, Kentucky. September 1940."

14/"Negro dock worker and son. New Orleans, Louisiana. March 1943."

15/Mrs. Mary Machado, her two daughters, her two grandchildren, and her great-grandchild. Gloucester, Massachusetts. June 1943.

16/"A group of Florida migratory workers on their way to Cranberry, New Jersey, to pick potatoes. Sawboro, North Carolina. July 1940."

17/"Levy Usher and his family plowing their two-acre tract in the community garden at Hazlehurst Farms. Hazlehurst, Georgia. April 1941."

18/"Mother of three soldiers. Placquemines Parish, Louisiana. June 1943."

19/"Mrs. Rose Carrendeno, Italian-American mother of six children. Three sons are in the armed forces. New York, New York. May 1943."

1/"Landing operations on Rendova Island, Solomon Islands, June 30, 1943. Attacking at the break of day in a heavy rainstorm, the first
Americans ashore huddle behind tree trunks and any other cover they can find."

World War Two: Pacific

2/"A group of F6F's attacking in support of the ground forces. Iwo Jima, 10:30 A.M. Altitude: 2,000 feet. February 21, 1945."

3/"A U.S. Marine charges across the beach on Peleliu Island, Palau Islands. March 1945."

4/"A U.S. Marine in action at Peleliu Island, Palau Islands. May 19, 1945."

5/"American troops, transferred from a Coast Guard–manned assault transport into a Coast Guard–manned landing craft, move in to attack the beach at Aitape in the Hollandia invasion. Helmeted and carrying fighting packs, these fighters catch their last smokes before the ramp drops on the enemy beach."

6/"An Army soldier catches his breath on Anguar Island, Palau Islands, between advances. March 19, 1945."

7/"A U.S. Marine on Peleliu Island, Palau Islands, waits for reinforcements before advancing. March 19, 1945."

8/"Marines resting after hunting snipers in caves along northern Saipan coastline near Marpi Point. July 10, 1944."

9/"These men have earned by bloody fighting the reputation of being skilled jungle fighters. They are U.S. Marine Rangers, gathered in front of a Jap dugout on Cape Totokina on Bougainville, . . . which they helped to take." January 5, 1944."

10/"Flames leaping into Japanese caves from an amphibious tractor on Peleliu as U.S. Marines advance slowly to block the Nips' escape. September 1944."

11/"Sprawled bodies on beach of Tarawa, testifying to ferocity of the struggle for this stretch of sand.
November 22, 1943."

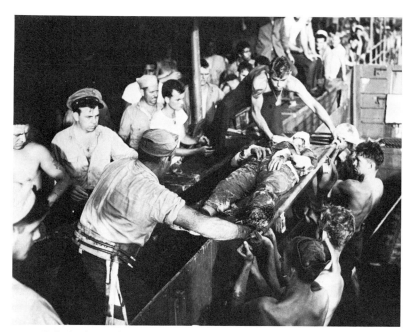

12/Medical care for wounded in the Saipan invasion. Wounded put aboard a Coast Guard–manned attack transport. June 24, 1944.

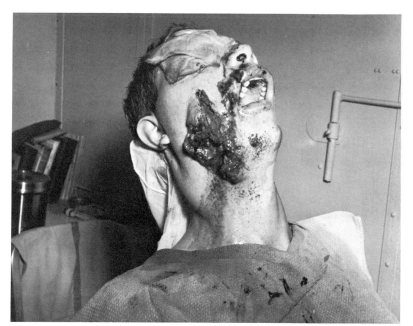

13/"Battle casualties of Iwo Jima, Volcano Islands, in Base Hospital #18 on Guam, for surgical treatment. April 6, 1945."

14/"Because of the many requests for baptism from Coast Guardsmen stationed at a remote Pacific base, Chaplain Harold G. Sanders selected this mountain pool for a weekly Sunday afternoon service. Approximately thirty servicemen are baptised there each Sunday, with the voices of the base choir adding to the solemnity of the occasion. Assisting Chaplain Sanders is Farley Archer, Coast Guardsman. September 29, 1944."

World War Two:
Europe

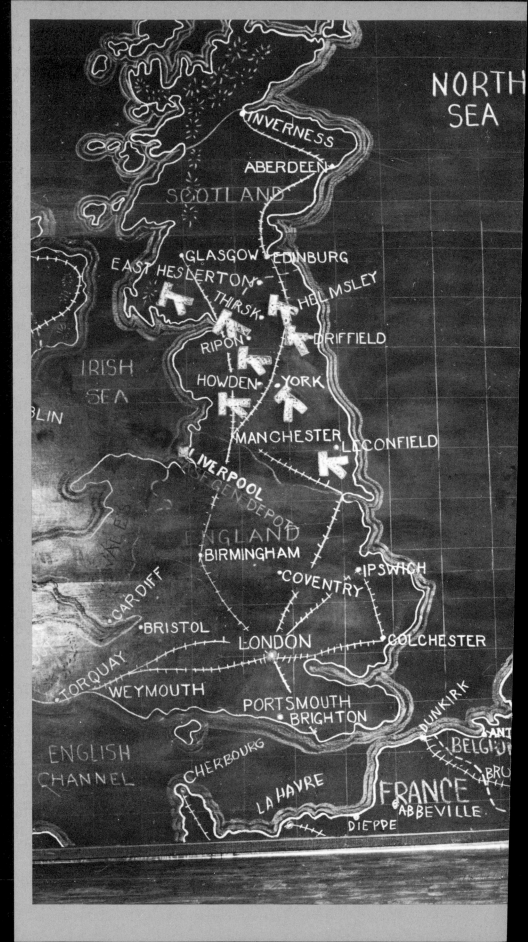

1/"Air service command. Instructor conducting a discussion at the staff command school. Warner Robins, Georgia. July 1943."

2/"No building in this section of Jakobsullesheim, Germany, remains intact. The town was taken by units of the 1st Division, U.S. First Army. February 28, 1945."

3/"30th Infantry, 3rd Division, U.S. 7th Army, searching for snipers. Zweibrucken, Germany. March 20, 1945."

4/"1st Battalion, 180th Inf. Reg., 45th Division. Bensheim, Germany. March 27, 1945."

5/"Wesel, Germany, focal point of attack of American forces as they crossed the Rhine north of the Ruhr Valley."

6/"The German was killed while hiding in the entrance of a garden in Cherbourg, France. June 27, 1944."

7/"House-to-house fighting, St. Malo, France. August 8, 1944."

8/"Combat engineers of the 6th Armored
Division 1252 Engr. Sup. U.S. 3rd Army,
pass through battle-scarred Dasburg,
Germany. February 22, 1945."

9/"'Death of a World.' Dead Nazis and destroyed towns are left behind
as the Allies battle their way through Germany. April 1945."

161

10/"Peace in Times Square."

11/"Liberated Polish inmates, Dachau."

12/"U.S. Medical Corpsman, 7th Army, looks into a train car. Dachau."

13/"Jewish slave labor, Neunburg atrocity."

14/"Civilians gaze upon the bodies of 800 Russians, Poles, Czechs. Namering, Germany."

15/"A dead Russian, reburied by citizens of Hanover near their town hall, under supervision of 35th Division, U.S. 9th Army. May 2, 1945."

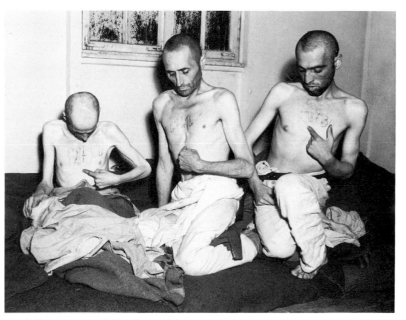

16/"Prisoners of Buchenwald point to their tattoos. May 1, 1945."

17/Nador Livia, a Jewish survivor of Gusen Concentration Camp. Before the war, she was a famous actress in Budapest.

18/"U.S. Senator Alben W. Barkley of Kentucky, chairman of the House-Senate Committee on War Crimes. Buchenwald, near Weimar, Germany. April 24, 1945."

Credits

In the following credits section, indicating the sources of the photographs appearing in the eighteen chapters of this book, certain abbreviations have been used in the interest of saving space: LC refers to the Library of Congress; NA to the National Archives.

The Civil War

1/LC-B811-570
2/LC-B813-1880
3/Lot 4191
4/LC-B813-1644
5/LC-B817-7483
6/LC-B817-7274
7/LC-B813-1555
8/LC-B817-7339
9/LC-B813-1489
10/LC-B811-4032
11/LC-B8184-B-527
12/LC-B815-580, Alex Gardner
13/LC-B8184-B-1292
14/LC-B8184-614
15/LC-USZ62-4695
16/LC-B8184-B-637
17/LC-B8184-558, Alex Gardner

The West

1/NA-106-WB-89
2/LC-USZ62-15578, J.C.H. Grabill
3/LC-D10848, Heyn & Matzen
4/LC-D10821, Heyn & Matzen
5/LC-Lot 4972-A, Edward S. Curtis
6/LC-Lot 4972-A, Edward S. Curtis
7/LC-Lot 4972-A, Edward S. Curtis
8/LC-USZ62-46735, J.C.H. Grabill
9/LC-USZ62-17591, J.C.H. Grabill
10/LC-USZ62-22483, J.C.H. Grabill
11/LC-USZ62-11769, J.C.H. Grabill

12/LC-USZ62-7120, J.C.H. Grabill
13/LC-USZ62-22477, J.C.H. Grabill
14/LC-USZ62-46188, J.C.H. Grabill
15/LC-USZ62-27931, J.C.H. Grabill
16/LC-USZ62-16251

Black Life

1/LC-J694-192, Frances Benjamin Johnston
2/LC-J694-230, Frances Benjamin Johnston
3/LC-Keystone View Co., B. L. Lingley
4/LC-Keystone View Co., B. L. Lingley
5/LC-D4-19395, Detroit Photographic Co.
6/LC-Keystone View Co., B. L. Lingley
7/LC-Alfred Campbell Co.
8/LC-J694-526, Frances Benjamin Johnston
9/LC-J694-535, Frances Benjamin Johnston
10/LC-J694-X4, Frances Benjamin Johnston
11/LC-J694-251, Frances Benjamin Johnston
12/LC-J694-302, Frances Benjamin Johnston
13/LC-J694-482, Frances Benjamin Johnston
14/LC-J694-162, Frances Benjamin Johnston
15/LC-USZ62-64712, Frances Benjamin Johnston
16/LC-J694-250, Frances Benjamin Johnston
17/LC-J694-250, Frances Benjamin Johnston
18/LC-USZ62-65770, Frances Benjamin Johnston

City Life

1/LC-USZ62-24063, Underhill Collection
2/LC-D4-16664, Detroit Photographic Co.
3/LC-USZ62-5426, S. Krausz
4/LC-USZ62-42634, S. Krausz
5/LC-USZ62-5422, S. Krausz
6/LC-USZ62-23643, S. Krausz
7/LC-USZ62-12617, S. Krausz
8/LC-USZ62-16278, S. Krausz
9/LC-D4-62021, Detroit Photographic Co.
10/LC-D4-018831, Detroit Photographic Co.

11/LC-USZ62-12989
12/Lot 10872-4, Bain Collection
13/LC-USZ62-67639, Byron Collection
14/LC-D4-71298, Detroit Photographic Co.
15/LC-USZ62-17137, Frances Benjamin Johnston
16/LC-C801-5, Charles H. Currier
17/LC-C801-171, Charles H. Currier

Industry and Agriculture

1/LC-D4-018671, Detroit Photographic Co.
2/LC-D4-19057, Detroit Photographic Co.
3/LC-D4-012557, Detroit Photographic Co.
4/LC-D4-019055, Detroit Photographic Co.
5/LC-D4-011587, Detroit Photographic Co.
6/LC-Keystone View Co., #22148
7/LC-Keystone View Co., #22142
8/LC-D4-14756, Detroit Photographic Co.
9/LC-USZ62-69833
10/LC-Keystone View Co.
11/LC-Keystone View Co.
12/LC-USZ62-56648
13/LC-Underwood & Underwood
14/LC-J698-100080, Frances Benjamin Johnston
15/LC-D4-12862, Detroit Photographic Co.
16/LC-USZ62-11850
17/LC-Lot 1107, Keystone View Co., #6702
18/LC-USZ62-60108, Underwood & Underwood
19/LC-D4-011474, Detroit Photographic Co.
20/LC-USZ62-34842
21/LC-USZ62-7311, White Stereo Co.
22/LC-D4-070681, Detroit Photographic Co.
23/LC-USZ62-52074, Keystone View Co.
24/LC-D4-019050, Detroit Photographic Co.
25/LC-USZ62-51195
26/LC-Single Picture File, "Cotton"
27/LC-Miscellaneous Subject File, "Farming"
28/LC-USZ62-19632
29/LC-Miscellaneous Subject File

Child Labor and Strikes

1/LC-B2-3553-13, Bain Collection
2/LC-Lot 7479, Vol. 6, Mills, #3653, Lewis Hine
3/LC-Lot 7476, Canneries, #2003, Lewis Hine
4/LC-USZ62-47514, Vol. 5, Mills, Lot 7479
5/LC-Lot 7475, Vol. 3, Agriculture, #4891
6/LC-Lot 7479, Vol. 5, Mills, #3112, Lewis Hine
7/LC-Lot 7479, Vol. 3, Mills #1813, Lewis Hine
8/LC-Lot 7477, Coal, #92, Lewis Hine
9/LC-B2-2369-13
10/LC-B2-969-6, Bain Collection
11/LC-B2-2082-5, Bain Collection
12/LC-USZ62-23413, Bain Collection

The Philippine Insurrection

1/LC-USZ62-41758, Dotter Collection
2/LC-USZ62-14542, Rockett Collection
3/LC-USZ62-14544, Rockett Collection
4/LC-USZ62-30299, Rockett Collection
5/LC-USZ62-46691, Rockett Collection
6/LC-USZ62-1253, Rockett Collection
7/LC-USZ61-955, Dotter Collection
8/LC-USZ62-30335, Rockett Collection
9/LC-Lot 5046, Rockett Collection
10/LC-USZ62-10405, Rockett Collection
11/LC-USZ62-41917, Dotter Collection
12/LC-Lot 10,157
13/LC-Lot 5596, Dotter Collection

Ideal and Comic Types

1/LC-Lot 9799, Frances Benjamin Johnston
2/LC-Lot 11147-1, Bain Collection
3/LC-Lot 10816, Bain Collection
4/LC-USZ62-50383, Erwin E. Smith Collection
5/LC-J698-90118, Frances Benjamin Johnston
6/LC-USZ62-76161, 33468
7/LC-White Stereo Co.
8/LC-Griffith & Griffith Co.
9/LC-J698-4987-G, Frances Benjamin Johnston
10/LC-White Stereo Co.
11/LC-Lot 7335, Standard Scenic View, #1668
12/LC-Griffith & Griffith Co.
13/LC-Lot 7329, American Stereo Co.
14/LC-J698-61043, Frances Benjamin Johnston
15/LC-Lot 7331/International View Co., #4027(b)
16/LC-Lot 7331/International View Co., #4028(c)
17/LC-Lot 7335, Standard Scenic Co., #1663(12)

Misfortunes

1/LC-USZ62-52432
2/LC-USZ62-49317
3/LC-USZ62-46831
4/LC-USZ62-75640
5/LC-Lot 8587
6/LC-USZ62-26560, E.W. Jones Stereo
7/LC-Lot 9964C, Blumberg

World War One

1/NA, U.S. Army Signal Corps, AU, 1651, Paul Thompson
2/NA, U.S. Army Signal Corps, A8218, Lt. Reid
3/NA, U.S. Army Signal Corps, A8217, Lt. Reid
4/NA, U.S. Army Signal Corps, A8219, Lt. Reid
5/NA, U.S. Army Signal Corps, 21000, Sgt. James L. McGarrigle
6/NA, U.S. Army Signal Corps, A21002, Sgt. James L. McGarrigle
7/NA, U.S. Army Signal Corps, EU 3070
8/NA, U.S. Army Signal Corps, E25357
9/NA, U.S. Army Signal Corps, A31, 7487
10/NA, U.S. Army Signal Corps, AU 5620
11/NA, U.S. Army Signal Corps, E25894 (also: 23675), Sgt. 1st Class J. T. Seabrook
12/NA, U.S. Army Signal Corps, E20909
13/NA, U.S. Army Signal Corps, E28554, Sgt. 1st Class Fineberg
14/NA, U.S. Army Signal Corps, 32158, neg. marked 32168, Lt. R. W. Sears
15/NA, U.S. Army Signal Corps, E14647
16/NA, U.S. Army Signal Corps, 13243, Sgt. 1st Class C. H. White
17/NA, U.S. Army Signal Corps, 4067
18/LC-Lot 7735
19/NA, U.S. Army Signal Corps, 153412, neg. marked 153413, Sgt. Spiegel

Women after the War

1/NA, Women's Bureau, 86-G-11F-7
2/NA, Women's Bureau, 86-G-3E-11, T. E. Meachum
3/NA, Women's Bureau, 86-G-3E-9
4/NA, Women's Bureau, 86-G-5J-6
5/LC-Lot 11542-1
6/LC-Lot 11542-1
7/NA, Women's Bureau, 86-G-2K-3

8/LC-Lot 11542-1
9/LC-Lot 11542-1

Farm Life

1/NA-RG33-SC6569
2/NA-RG33-SC5585
3/NA-RG33-SC9276
4/NA-RG33-SC7822
5/NA-RG33-SC9276
6/NA-RG33-SC6683
7/NA-RG33-SC11182
8/NA-RG33-SC5825
9/NA-RG33-SC1241
10/NA-RG33-SC11870
11/NA-RG33-SC11868
12/NA-RG16, 16-G-162-2-SC6765, G. W. Ackerman
13/NA-RG33-SC10822

The Depression

1/LC-USF34-29598-D, Arthur Rothstein
2/LC-USF34-20583-C, Dorothea Lange
3/LC-USF34-17957-C, Dorothea Lange
4/LC-USF33-11153-M4, Russell Lee
5/LC-USF34-17956-C, Dorothea Lange
6/LC-USF33-6071-M4, Ben Shahn
7/LC-USF34-8594-D, John Vachon
8/LC-USF33-12275-M5, Russell Lee
9/LC-5169-M4, Edwin Rosskam
10/LC-USF34-52710-D
11/LC-USF34-9575-C, Dorothea Lange
12/LC-USF34-32742-D, Russell Lee
13/LC-USF33-2945-M2, Arthur Rothstein
14/LC-USF342-8032A, Walker Evans
15/LC-USF33-30577-M2, Marion Post Wolcott
16/LC-USF33-1433-M2, John Vachon
17/LC-USF341-11299-B, Paul Carter
18/LC-USF342-8164-A, Walker Evans
19/LC-8939-D, John Vachon
20/LC-USF34-18216-E, Dorothea Lange
21/LC-8760-D, John Vachon
22/LC-USF33-11661-M2, Russell Lee
23/LC-USF34-40376-D, Sheldon Dick
24/LC-USF33-11770-M4, Russell Lee
25/LC-USF34-52649-D, Marion Post Wolcott

War Mobilization

1/LC-USW3-26388-D, Arthur Siegel
2/LC-USF34-71214-D, Russell Lee
3/16216-M2, John Vachon

4/LC-USW3-22900-E, John Vachon
5/LC-USW3-1570-D, Mead Maddick Lownds
6/LC-USW3-16248-C, Arthur Siegel
7/7119-2A, Gen'l Motors Corp., LC-USZ62-37328
8/1569-D, Mead Maddick Lownds,
    LC-USZ62-58915
9/LC-USW3-34936-D, Jack Delano

Workers and Citizens

1/LC-USW3-34451-D, John Vachon
2/LC-USW3-25890-D, Arthur Siegel
3/LC-USW3-6582-D, Arthur Rothstein
4/LC-USF34-83184-C, John Collier
5/LC-USF34-24521-D, Arthur Rothstein
6/LC-USW3-26320-D, Arthur Siegel
7/LC-USW3-3108-D, Arthur Rothstein
8/LC-USF34-43113-D, Jack Delano
9/LC-USF34-41255-D, Jack Delano
10/LC-USF34-24524-D, Arthur Rothstein
11/LC-USF34-29297-D, Arthur Rothstein
12/LC-USF34-29282-D, Arthur Rothstein
13/LC-USF34-29506-D, Arthur Rothstein
14/LC-USF34-26899-D, Arthur Rothstein
15/LC-USF34-24527-D, Arthur Rothstein

Romance and Family Life

1/LC-USW3-23904-D, Marjory Collins

2/LC-USW3-28903-D, Marjory Collins
3/LC-USF34-61340-D, John Vachon
4/LC-USF34-61014-D, John Vachon
5/LC-USW3-7396-D, Arthur Rothstein
6/LC-USF33-3622-MI, Arthur Rothstein
7/LC-USF34-56906-E, Marion Post Wolcott
8/LC-USW3-3880-D, Arthur Rothstein
9/LC-USF34-36865-D, Russell Lee
10/LC-USW3-23095-E, Esther Bubley
11/LC-USW3-21005E, Esther Bubley
12/LC-USF34-13432-C, Gordon R. Parks
13/LC-USF34-56110-D, Marion Post Wolcott
14/LC-USW3-22841-E, John Vachon
15/LC-USW3-31668-C, Gordon Parks
16/LC-USF34-40820-D, Jack Delano
17/LC-USF34-43759-D, Jack Delano
18/LC-USW3-33962-D, John Vachon
19/LC-USW3-30282-D, Gordon Parks

World War Two: Pacific

1/NA, U.S. Navy
2/NA, U.S. Navy, #CV-10 288-6
3/NA, U.S. Navy, #48359
4/NA, U.S. Navy, #48358
5/NA, U.S. Coast Guard, #177381
6/NA, U.S. Navy, #48355
7/NA, U.S. Navy, #48354
8/NA, U.S. Navy, #287226

9/NA, U.S. Navy, #205686
10/NA, U.S. Navy, #272912
11/NA, U.S. Navy, #57405
12/NA, U.S. Coast Guard, #234277
13/NA, U.S. Navy, #311496
14/NA, U.S. Coast Guard, #281647

World War Two: Europe

1/LC-USW3-35554-D, Jack Delano
2/Pentagon, U.S. Army Signal Corps, SC201526
3/Pentagon, U.S. Army Signal Corps, SC202746
4/Pentagon, U.S. Army Signal Corps, SC204729
5/LC-Lot 10422, U.S. Army, Air Force photo
    #56831AC
6/Pentagon, U.S. Army Signal Corps, SC193970
7/Pentagon, U.S. Army Signal Corps, SC192697
8/Pentagon, U.S. Army Signal Corps, SC201311
9/Pentagon, U.S. Army Signal Corps, SC203411
10/NA-208-N-40921
11/NA-208-AA-206J1
12/NA-208-AA-129H-18
13/Pentagon, U.S. Army Signal Corps, SC206185
14/Pentagon, U.S. Army Signal Corps, SC206914
15/Pentagon, U.S. Army Signal Corps, SC205627
16/Pentagon, U.S. Army Signal Corps, SC205489
17/Pentagon, U.S. Army Signal Corps,
    SC204810-S
18/Pentagon, U.S. Army Signal Corps, SC204745

About the Author

Michael Lesy was educated in Ohio and then went on
to Columbia University and the University
of Wisconsin. He received his doctorate in American History from
Rutgers University, and has continued his work as a photographer/historian
in his last three books, *Wisconsin Death Trip,*
Real Life: Louisville in the Twenties,
and *Time Frames.*

A Note About the Type

The text of this book was set in Nicolas Cochin, a typeface
named for Charles Nicolas Cochin, the younger,
an eighteenth-century French engraver. It is an original and commendable
effort to reproduce the copperplate lettering used to caption
the engravings of the period.

Composed by Centennial Graphics, Inc., Ephrata, Pennsylvania
Printed and bound by The Murray Printing Company, Westford, Massachusetts
Production and manufacturing: Kathy Grasso
Copyediting: Lorraine Alexander Veach
Editorial coordination: Sona Vogel
Book design and layout: Susan Mitchell